PAM

The life & loves of
PAMELA ANDERSON

By Pat Riordan

Edited by Nicholas Maier

AMI
BOOKS

American Media, Inc.

PAM
The life and loves of Pamela Anderson

Copyright © 2003 AMI Books, Inc.

Cover design: Carlos Plaza
Interior design: Debbie Browning

ISBN: 1-932270-08-6

First printing: June 2003

Printed in the United States of America

10 9 8 7 6 5 4 3 2 1

Introduction

IMAGINE PAMELA ANDERSON NAKED — it's easy if you try.

Maybe you've already seen her that way, enthusiastically doing the nasty with tattooed heavy metal bad boys in one of those two infamous XXX-rated videotapes or posing nude in the pages of Playboy in one of her record-breaking 10 pictorials. You might have come across Pamela wearing nothing but her birthday suit in anti-fur ads for People for the Ethical Treatment of Animals or seen her in the buff on one of hundreds of thousands of Web sites on the Internet. At the very least, you have seen her spilling out of ultratight dresses in newspapers and magazines, at awards ceremonies and on her own syndicated action-comedy TV show, V.I.P. And you'd have to be a blind nun living in Antarctica to have missed her in a second-skin one-piece red Speedo on Baywatch.

Pamela Anderson may be the most famous woman to take her clothes off since Lady Godiva or Marilyn Monroe. It has been her ticket out of a dull life in a small town in Canada to the blinding limelight of Hollywood. It is not just an act; she has confessed to doing her housework and swinging on trapezes in the raw. For Pamela, nudity means freedom. And, of course, fame and fortune.

So it was no surprise that in the fall of 2002,

Pamela Anderson found herself stark naked once again. This time she was getting ready to put on a bikini and bounce back to the beach in the latest Baywatch reunion TV spectacular. It probably wasn't what she was hoping for in the way of her next acting job, however. After leaving the show in 1997 and thoroughly shocking David Hasselhoff, the star and part owner of Baywatch, with her kinky escapades, Pamela decided not to look back.

Few observers gave her the credit she deserved for creating and starring in V.I.P., even though at one point it outranked Baywatch in the ratings. Pamela Anderson was mostly known as the pinup with the enhanced breasts, the homemade-video porn star, the wife of hard-partying Motley Crue drummer Tommy Lee, the woman who had her violent, abusive husband arrested for slapping her around, the divorcee and working single mom fighting a nasty custody battle for her two sons. It hardly mattered what she did as an actress. Each new scandal, each candid confession, secured her status as the sexiest and most notorious woman in the universe.

After V.I.P. came to an end, Pamela met a new man, Bob Ritchie, a raunchy singer and rapper from Detroit who performed on stage with strippers and recorded under the name Kid Rock. They had gotten engaged and she had planned to retire from show business to concentrate on being a mom to her two sons, Brandon and Dylan. But Pamela's divorce and custody battles with Tommy Lee were financially punishing. After turning down David Hasselhoff twice, the blonde dropped the bombshell: She would appear for three days work on the three-week location shoot in exchange for half a million dollars. In order to meet her demands, Hasselhoff persuaded Pamela's co-stars to take a cut in pay.

The signed contract proved to be worth every penny — including the extra cash it took to get Pamela on a chartered jet to Hawaii when she missed her original flight — because without her, the show would not only not go on, it wouldn't even get made. Reprising her role as Baywatch's spacey but sweet CJ Parker, who now owned a bar and grill in Hawaii, was going to be a day at the beach. Pamela would no longer be a lifeguard, racing across the sand and plunging into the surf in slow motion, the camera trained on her every jiggle, but there was no question that she would be showing plenty of skin in an orange bikini.

Pamela must have been glad it wasn't the famous red bathing suit. There were too many memories, particularly one from the spring of 2001, when a female stalker snuck into the house and spent a night sleeping in a guest bedroom down the hall from Pamela and her kids. When she was discovered, the intruder handed the housekeeper a note. It clearly spelled out that the stalker was dangerously obsessed with Pamela and possibly suicidal. Pamela called the cops and when they arrested the woman, she was covered in grime and scabs and wearing a red Baywatch bathing suit.

All these things likely raced through Pamela's active imagination as she stood there naked, getting ready to join the rest of the Baywatch gang for the reunion special. This was not something she had ever intended to do again, but history has a way of repeating itself. Pam grew up in a household with drinking and domestic violence, always telling herself that she could never, ever be with a man who hit her, but some of the men she went out with did. She allowed one boyfriend to film their most intimate moments, then made another sex tape on her honeymoon. She had breast implants to bolster an already spectacular figure, took them out and then put them back in again. She filed for divorce, changed her mind, filed again and reconciled one more time before finally crawling away from the wreckage of her marriage to Tommy Lee.

Despite all of the terrible things that have happened to her, all the spontaneous decisions she made that turned out to be unwise, Pamela Anderson knows how to turn life's lemons into lemonade. Trying to put a spin on all the success she has had and all the sadness and regret she has felt deep inside, she believes that all of it — the happiness and the heartache — is a part of her journey through life. Inclined to practice a multi-faceted spirituality rather than a specific religious doctrine, Pam nonetheless believes that "God never gives me more than I can handle."

"I've learned through therapy that you have choices that can instantly change your life," she once said. "So now if I have a negative thought, I give myself 15 seconds to take it back. Or else you have to deal with the karma police."

Fame and wealth, Pamela believed, could never insulate her from making mistakes. "I'm one of those people where it doesn't take a brick to fall on my head," she confides. "Just a building." But when that happens, it's all about learning lessons, getting back up, dusting herself off and starting over again.

The latest building to fall was the biggest and most devastating. It made headlines around the world and gave Pam another cause to throw herself into, another misconception to clear up, another wrong to right. This time it was personal and a matter of life and death. Someone had leaked to the press that she had tested positive for the antibodies to hepatitis C, the chronic disease that can cause fatal liver failure. Country singer Naomi Judd had announced her retirement from the stage due to this blood-borne disease in 1990, but when you are Pamela Anderson, people have a tendency to assume the worst. They speculated that it had happened during her breast enhancement surgeries or that it was sexually transmitted. In fact, she claimed that the infection came from sharing a tattoo needle with Tommy Lee, whom she loved and trusted, who had hepatitis C and never told her. He, in turn, publicly denied it all, also claiming that in all his years as a rock star, he had never caught a sexually transmitted disease.

Until then Pamela had been just one of the 170 million people in the world living quietly with the infection. She had known for a while and, having long been an advocate of good nutrition and exercise, she was in good health. Now, in the midst of a lengthy and bitter battle for the custody of her children, it had become public, and the awful implication was that she was not fit to be a mother, that she had gotten what she deserved and was going to die. Looking at herself naked that day in her dressing room in Hawaii, Pam must have wondered how the beautiful, bountiful body that had brought her so far, so fast, could be in mortal danger.

It may have taken a full 15 seconds for Pamela Anderson to take back that frightening thought — to reword it, to accept the unacceptable and still find the strength to stay alive. She needed to for her kids, who are her life, for her fiancé, Kid Rock, her family, her friends, her fans, and last, but certainly not least, for herself.

Chapter 1

ON THE DAY THAT she was born, Pamela Denise Anderson became an instant star. It was July 1, 1967 — the 100th anniversary of Canada — and the daughter of Barry and Carol Anderson was the first centennial baby in Ladysmith, a small town on Vancouver Island in British Columbia. A local photographer thought she was such a pretty newborn that he published her picture in the town newspaper.

If you believe in things like destiny and symbolism, as Pamela Anderson does, then she was certainly born on a significant day. She shares her birthday with Deborah Harry, the vivacious lead singer of Blondie, who merged punk and pop and became an alternative kind of sex goddess. Her birthday is the same as Dan Aykroyd, a fellow Canadian and comedian, as well as Princess Diana, the most photographed and talked about woman in the world. Pamela Anderson was born a Cancer ruled by the sign of the crab. It's the most domestic of all the zodiac signs, the one that moves sideways through the sands of time and crawls over the rocks in the streams of life. Hard on the outside, sweet and fleshy when out of its shell, the Cancer crab is always looking for a safe and loving home.

When Pamela was just a young babe, the

Andersons moved to Comox, a small fishing village with a population of 6,000. They lived in a three-room cabin, perched on a bluff overlooking the Pacific Ocean on the coast of Vancouver Island. Carol and Barry married when he was 19 and she was 17. They had Pam soon after.

The Andersons struggled financially. Four years later, it would get even tougher when Pam's baby brother Gerry was born. Carol waited tables at Smitty's pancake house and frequently held a second job to buy her kids clothes from the Sears catalog. Barry had a furnace servicing business. He used to drive Pamela around in a truck that she remembered as "this big hillbilly wagon." Embarrassed to be seen in it, she used to jump out and walk the last couple of blocks to school.

From the get-go, Pamela was a handful. She once smeared the family cat in butter and spices and put it in the oven. On another occasion, she hid her baby brother, Gerry, with whom she had to share a room, inside a barrel and then "alerted the whole town that he was missing." She was a high-spirited girl who used to take spoons out of her mother's pantry and try to dig holes in the yard that would lead her to China. Pamela wanted to join the circus, which may explain a taste she developed later for swings and trapezes. "If I could hang upside down most of the day," she once confessed, "I'd be very happy."

All that energy had its downside, however. She has said that she did not come equipped with a "shut-off valve" and when she got excited or stressed she hyperventilated and fainted. That happened a lot. "I was a three o'clock in the morning-nightmare child," she admitted.

A penchant for drama led her to voice personal opinions without inhibition. "They called me STPP — Stir The Pot Pam — when I was little," she confessed. Despite the incident with the family cat, she was an animal lover and hated the fact that her father hunted. "I threw a huge stink and threw myself in front of the truck." It did the trick; Barry gave up hunting. It wouldn't be the last time Pamela vexed her father. During one show-and-tell session at school, she invited her class to her house with the promise that her father would take them ice skating. For a day she was exceedingly popular — until the kids actually showed up at the house and discovered that Pamela hadn't bothered to tell her father. Later, when she was asked what prepared her for acting, she replied, "Being a compulsive liar when I was a kid."

Though she now enjoys a close relationship with her father, the fact is that when Pamela was growing up, Barry Anderson was not a particularly understanding man. Pamela didn't have a lot of dolls, like some girls, but she did have a treasured stuffed animal, an alligator, whose teeth she had darkened with a Magic Marker. She called him Tigger. One day she was looking for her toy and noticed that her dad had stuffed it in a hole in the dryer vent in their garage.

Many of the problems came from the fact that Barry was a hard drinker and Pamela would often come home to find him passed out on the porch. That drinking inevitably ignited his temper. Mostly, Barry took things out on his wife. Sometimes it turned physical. "Seeing your mother being hurt is the most traumatic thing," Pamela admitted. She remembers her mother crying in the bathroom and her brother hiding and that left her to stand up to her father. Once, Pam even punched him in the chin. "I was pretty ballsy. I was the one who was yelling at my dad and then running for the door."

It was then that she would take off and visit her grandfather, Barry's dad Herman. Pamela's grandpa was from Helsinki, Finland. He worked as a logger but had an intellectual streak. He wrote poetry, read philosophy, kept a journal of his dreams and gave his granddaughter books to read. One was called Your Body & How It Works, which led her down the road of good nutrition and regular exercise. "You are your empire, your body is your temple," Gramps would tell her. "Just take every opportunity as it comes."

Pamela's mother would later tell her daughter that her beloved grandfather had passed on his alcoholism and abusive personality to Pam's father. But that was not the Gramps Pamela knew. Perhaps he was hoping to find redemption, to be the kindly man for his granddaughter that he could not be for his own son. Pamela's grandfather would always say, "You're a brand-new life. You're not an extension of your parents. Do what you want to do and be a good person, and things will come to you."

Grandpa knew what was going on at home and he knew that stress played a huge role in good health and that heart disease and alcoholism ran on both sides of Pam's family. He used to tell his granddaughter that when things got tense at home she should go to the beach and meditate. "He used to say, 'take a rock and really become the rock,'" Pamela explained. "I mean it sounds kind of kooky, but it really helped me through a lot when I was little." The greatest gift he gave her, however, was the gift of having a dream. He encouraged her to think big, saying that she didn't have to be a smalltown girl all her life.

That was what Pamela was, a small girl in a small town and there wasn't much understanding for a child like her then and there. The concept of "the tweens," that sometimes troublesome age between

10 and 12 when a youngster is no longer a child, but not quite a teenager, didn't really have a name when Pamela was in her preadolescence. But she suffered through it nonetheless. During that time, she tried shoplifting, as a lot of kids do, and got caught stealing Bonne Bell bubble-gum lip gloss.

This troublesome age would become more acute when, suddenly, at the age of 61, Pamela's grandfather, the man who gave her support and love, who taught her the value of poetry and literature and dreams, passed away. Pamela, 11, did not go to the funeral. It was Gramps' last wish, wanting to spare Pam from any further sorrow. Even now she doesn't like funerals.

No man would ever fill her beloved grandfather's place in Pamela's heart. Still, she was not immune to the charms of the opposite sex. Her first crush, dating all the way back to kindergarten, was on a boy with big ears named Donald. She moved on to Matthew and Kenny and learned how to make the two boys jealous. Kissing one of them brought both of them to blows. Pam was 5 years old at the time when she realized she had the power to cause boys to fight over her.

Pamela recalls her first serious kiss with distaste. She was in the fifth grade and she wondered what the big deal was, why everyone she knew was raving about it. "This guy jammed his tongue so far down my throat," she told Playboy, "that I avoided kissing people for a long time after that."

There was another kiss, one that she will never forget, as hard as she tries. Pamela was 12, already looking very grown up, yet still completely innocent. That innocence was about to be lost forever, against her wishes and with brute force.

Chapter 2

FOR 20 YEARS, PAMELA Anderson lived with a horrible secret: When she was only 12 years old, she was overpowered and raped by a man who viciously took her virginity and threatened to harm her afterward to make sure she would not tell. Fearing for her life, she did not report him to the authorities and in the years that passed only shared the awful truth with a few close confidants.

But in early 1999, Pamela went public about the incident while appearing as a guest on shock jock Howard Stern's radio show. It was a terrifying story she felt sure she would take to her grave, hardly the kind of thing she ever thought she'd reveal to Howard Stern. Pamela had been a frequent visitor to Stern's studio and happily engaged in the bawdy banter that has made him famous. But on this particular visit, Pamela was feeling vulnerable. Just one year ago, her husband, Tommy Lee, had attacked her while she was holding her son. And she had recently returned from a trip to Uruguay to promote her TV show, V.I.P., where she had been surrounded by a pack of teenage boys who made lewd comments, then groped and fondled her.

Something Stern said that day unleashed a torrent of emotion in Pamela and she blurted out the painful details. The attack occurred in 1979, when she and a 13-year-old friend went to visit two older men at their home in Comox, British Columbia. The girl was a little bit more experienced than Pamela, but Pamela knew one of the men, and thought it would be harmless to go to their place for a game of backgammon. "That sounded OK to me, even though he was about 25," she recalled.

Shortly after the girls arrived, however, Pamela's friend went upstairs with one of the guys. Pamela didn't know what her friend was doing and was now alone with the other man. They began to play backgammon, but it was soon evident that he had something else on his mind. He kissed her. She was a little embarrassed because she had never been kissed that way before. She asked him to stop, but he wouldn't. Pamela begged, but he was bigger than her and much stronger. "I didn't have a chance," she remembered. "Before I could stop him, he pushed me on the couch. He was trying to pull my underpants down. He put his hand over my mouth and I couldn't scream. I even tried to bite him to make him stop, but he forced himself on me." He didn't listen to her pleas and he didn't care that she was crying. "At first I was numb, then I was in a state of shock, bleeding and agonized."

Still reeling with pain, Pamela listened in horror as her attacker warned her that if she told anyone, she would be disgraced. He was a cunning bastard who knew how to confuse and frighten a 12-year-old innocent. He spun a tale that left her convinced that if she made any kind of fuss, the word would get around in their small town and Pamela and her parents would never live down the shame. Then, "he threatened that if I ever told anyone, I'd end up at the bottom of the sea."

Pamela swore she wouldn't say a word. She was a terrified young girl and did not live in a supportive environment. There could be no guarantees for her safety or for justice being done if she went to the police. Would they believe her? Or would they try to twist it around so that it seemed like it was all her fault? The perpetrator had not only stolen her virtue, but had wreaked havoc on her psyche, leaving Pamela with scars that might never heal. Once thing was certain: She would never be as trusting again.

"He hurt me a lot taking my virginity," Pamela revealed. "For a long time I was frightened at the thought of sex. I just connected the act with fear and pain. It was an ugly experience I'll never forget." Nor would she forgive. She once told a friend, "I've often thought of going back there with a couple of tough guys and really having him worked over. But it wouldn't help. The damage was done."

Even the less-than-sensitive Howard Stern knew what that damage was. On the day that Pamela

Anderson recounted her horrible rape, he asked whether it might explain why she was attracted to violent men like her ex-husband Tommy Lee.

"Maybe," she replied. "Who knows?"

After the rape, Pamela fought to gain control of what then seemed like an unsafe world. Some victims shut down after such an experience, becoming loners plagued with shame and guilt, responses that create doubt and low self-esteem in rape victims. Pamela was no exception.

You wouldn't have guessed that if you knew her back then, however. On the outside she appeared to be a happy, popular teenager. Unlike a lot of young women who live with the stigma of rape, Pamela took a slightly different path when it came to coping with the trauma. She became an overachiever — Little Miss Extracurricular. It kept her away from the alienation she felt at home and helped her forget about the troubling feelings of victimization.

In school, Pamela was a straight-A student, played saxophone for seven years in the school's jazz band, sang in choir and did gymnastics. She was on the volleyball team, playing setter because she was only 5-feet-5-inches tall. "Even though she was the shortest girl, she had so much heart and determination that she became our star player," remembers her coach Pat Lewis.

Being athletic gave her physical strength and helped her feel empowered, which made her feel better about herself. Soon a more extroverted side of Pamela began to blossom, along with her figure. Although she once claimed that she didn't get her period until she was 18 — which she blamed on playing sports — Pamela had begun to fill out. "I went completely nuts as soon as I started to get hips and curves," she recalled. "Even though I was shy, I was wearing those dresses and going out with a bunch of different guys."

Her brother Gerry corroborated Pamela's popularity in her biography on the Web site he managed for her in the late '90s. "They nicknamed her Popcorn, because she would kind of hop when she was running from the boys." Due to her interest in athletics, she met a lot of jocks. The dating pool wasn't all that sophisticated. "Rugby was huge where I grew up," Pam remembered. "And very violent. You knew you had a good boyfriend if, like, half of his ear was missing."

Pam's first serious boyfriend was named Tyrone Anderson. They met at Highland Secondary School in Comox. She was 15 at the time and he was pretty insistent about having sex. It had only been three years since Pam was raped and she had no real interest, but consented nonetheless. "He was desperate to do it," Pam has said. "It was pretty awful. We did it in the car five or six times in four hours. Each time it lasted a few seconds and it wasn't great. I thought it was overrated."

However, over the six years they were together, they both learned how to enjoy it.

Tyrone recalled that Pamela came out of her cocoon when they were together. "It seemed as if our love affair stirred up the deep emotions inside her. Once we started sleeping together, she went from being a kid to a passionate woman. She became hungry for almost every experience that life could offer her. We promised to stay with each other forever — we were madly in love. We planned to marry and have kids and that's all I ever wanted."

At age 17, they were engaged and for a time even lived together. But it was not a bed of roses. "The more sensational she looked," Tyrone admitted, "the more possessive I became." It wasn't just jealousy that led to harsh words; Tyrone was physically abusive. "One time, he threw me out of a moving car," Pamela recalled. "I thought we would end up killing each other."

Even so, Pamela clung to the delusion that he still loved her. Perhaps, growing up with family violence and abuse, she didn't know that boyfriends weren't supposed to do things like that. Perhaps she thought he was better than what she had known before and that was all that she deserved. Perhaps she thought that deep down inside he really loved her and there must be something wrong with her that caused him to lash out. Whatever her reasoning, Pamela was terrified that he would leave her.

When Tyrone finally did leave town, to look for work in Red Deer, Alberta, some 800 miles away, Pamela decided to send him a reminder of what he was missing back home. She was 18 and incredibly fit, though hardly the centerfold she would become, when she posed for her first set of erotic photos. The photographer recalled that Pam "felt awkward about her body at first but came to life once she was in front of the camera. She often said she wanted to be a model — and she certainly proved she had what it takes."

In the first photo, she wore a low-cut black lace teddy with garters and stockings. Then she changed into white. Finally, she took a blue towel and artfully arranged it over her naked body, revealing her cleavage, navel and shapely legs. When it came time to drop the pictures off for processing, she was so nervous that she took them to a neighboring town and paid a boy to pick them up for her. Then she chose her favorites and sent them off to Tyrone.

It would be the first, but not the last time, that pictures of Pamela Anderson drove a man wild with desire.

Chapter 3

AFTER TAKING THOSE FIRST sexy photographs, Pamela felt a sense of exhilaration. Here was something that she liked doing. Maybe it could become a career.

She had already decided that she was not destined to become Mrs. Tyrone Anderson. Sure, she summoned up the courage to send him those pictures and they had produced the desired effect, but during the time when they were apart, Pamela began thinking about the relationship and wondering whether it was worth it. She started asking herself tough questions: Would this be just another lull in their stormy relationship? Would the rest of her life start to resemble her mother's? Would she spend the rest of her life married and miserable in a small Canadian town?

Pamela thought about what her grandfather always said, that she could mold her own destiny by opening the door when opportunity knocked. When she graduated from high school she filled out a questionnaire for the yearbook. Under "Desired Destiny" she scribbled "stewardess." Under "Probable Destiny" she prophetically wrote "California Beach Bum." Pamela instinctively felt that she would be doing a disservice to her grandpa's memory and to herself if she didn't heed the inner voice that told her to take the first steps in shaping her own destiny. She knew that the rest of her life would begin the moment she decided to break it off with Tyrone — and get the hell out of Comox.

By the time she turned 21, Pamela had left Vancouver Island. She packed up her things and took the ferry across the Strait of Georgia, leaving her small town for the big city of Vancouver. Even in 1988, Vancouver was a far more sophisticated city than Pamela had ever seen. There was a world of opportunity there in the city that is, for all intents and purposes, the Los Angeles of Canada. There were modeling and advertising agencies, television and film studios and all kinds of places where a pretty girl might get noticed.

One thing Pam realized right away is that the women in Vancouver looked a lot more stylish and polished. She might have been one of the prettiest girls in Comox, but in Vancouver she had some serious competition. The first thing she did was fix her hair. In Comox, she had worn it full, in an outdated Farrah Fawcett shag, and kept her natural color, a mousy brown. Eventually, she added blond highlights with teased bangs and long hair in the back. Then, when she moved to Vancouver, Pamela went blonde and adopted a more contemporary style.

There was no question that Pamela was beautiful and she still harbored dreams of becoming a model. Pamela had taken a job as a fitness instructor at a local gym and she was in such good shape that she was frequently approached for modeling jobs. Unfortunately, Pamela was a good three inches too short — and a little too girl-next-door cute — for the high fashion world of runways and magazine layouts. But her 34-C bust, tiny waist and shapely legs were absolutely perfect for swimsuits and workout gear, and her blue eyes, freckled button nose and newly golden hair gave her a sexy, healthy beach bunny look.

When she wasn't posing for photographs, Pamela did in-store promotions. The summer she turned 21, she landed a job selling Corona beer T-shirts. Her supervisor, Tim Coupland, who had the Corona license in Vancouver, remembers Pamela as an extremely successful sales associate. "We'd go into a grocery store with about 300 Corona T-shirts and set up a booth with Pam wearing a cutoff T-shirt and a pair of shorts. The sales were terrific. The only problem was that a lot of the guys in the stores started hanging around Pam in the booth all the time and a lot of the housewives who came in complained about it."

Coupland also offered Pam modeling assignments for California bathing suit lines he was promoting in British Columbia, but she had a problem with tardiness. "She was a nice enough girl, but I never thought she'd amount to anything back when she worked for me as a model," Coupland recalled. "I told her at the time, 'If you don't start showing up on time you'll end up cooking on a freighter some-where.' Boy, was I ever wrong."

In fact, Pamela's next gig wasn't as a cook at all. It turned out to be for a rival brewery and it wasn't even a job she was looking for. She got the job quite by accident, without an audition, and it would turn out to be her first appearance on televi-sion and the lucky break that really got her career in showbiz going.

In her years as a star, Pamela Anderson has lit up a lot of TV screens, from Baywatch to her explicit honeymoon video to her series V.I.P. But none of that would ever have happened if she hadn't caught the eye of a cameraman at a football game. The story has been told so many times that it's taken on the proportions of a myth, like Lana Turner being discovered at Schwab's drugstore — but it actually happened exactly this way:

Pamela was living next door to some friendly folks who happened to have an extra ticket to a BC Lions football game. She wasn't really a big fan of the sport; they hadn't played it much in Comox where she grew up, but when her neighbors offered to take her to a game, she figured why not? The neighbors also offered her a T-shirt that advertised

Labatt's Blue, a Canadian beer. Pam had enough experience modeling beer T-shirts to know that she'd look very good in it.

It was 1988, big hair was still in style and big bust lines had never gone out. Pamela had both and when the cameraman picked her out in the crowd, jumping up and down, cheering on her team, it only took a second for her image to be flashed up on the big screen of a JumboTron. The crowd went nuts. Before she even knew what was happening, Pamela was brought down to the 50-yard line as 50,000 people screamed their approval. Pamela had one fleeting thought in her head as she saw herself on that big screen, "God, I look old," she would recall much later.

However she felt, everyone else thought she looked terrific and a star was born. She became known as the Labatt's "Blue Zone Girl." The game was actually sponsored by Foster's lager, Pamela would later inform people, so Labatt's was obviously very pleased to get all the free publicity. It didn't take them long to find Pamela and sign her up to be their official model. That meant a lot of sessions with a photographer named Dan Ilicic. The pictures he took wound up on posters and bus shelter ads; Pamela wound up dating Dan.

Pamela's modeling career was suddenly going great guns. Her face was everywhere you looked and so was she. She was beginning to experience the thrill of being a celebrity, even if it was on a small scale. One day, while watching a friend at a fashion show in Vancouver, a rep from Playboy approached Pamela. The magazine had seen her Labatt's Blue Zone ad and had another, bluer shoot in mind. Her boyfriend, Dan Ilicic, put his foot down. Absolutely not, he said. Suddenly, he had become very protective of his Pygmalion. But the jealous photographer had only himself to blame — thanks to him, Pamela's portfolio was making the rounds.

Playboy called again, this time tracking Pamela down at home, and they were now offering her the cover of the magazine. Pamela recalled that she and Dan were fighting when the phone rang. He was yelling at her because she was watching some cute guy on TV. She asked how much she'd get paid; they said they'd let her know. Triumphantly, she told her boyfriend that if they called her back she would say yes. "The worst thing you can do is tell me not to do something," Pamela has often said. Dan was furious, throwing things around the room.

Pam, on the other hand, was absolutely calm. She may have been a babe, but she was no babe in the woods and she knew what exposure in Playboy could do for a girl. She had seen an issue of her father's back in Comox and remembered it as taste-ful, even beautiful. And her red-blooded boyfriend

Dan had copies of Playboy, too. She remembers thinking it was weird that he thought Playboy was so great but she was not allowed to be in it.

A few days after that phone call from Playboy, Pamela discovered just how deep Dan's double standards ran. Pamela and Dan had become engaged, but he was secretly taking a shot at another blonde, two-timing his fiancée. She'd already bought a wedding dress and even sent out invitations, the ceremony only two weeks away. Pamela picked up the phone and called Playboy. Were they still interested, she inquired?

Chapter 4

WAS PLAYBOY STILL INTERESTED? "I immediately brought her down for a cover shoot," recalled Playboy's West Coast photo editor, Marilyn Grabowski. "Of course, I had an ulterior motive in mind; Pamela would be a brilliant choice for a Playmate. It wasn't my practice to bring girls into town for cover shootings; we had so many beautiful girls living in L.A., it was like bringing coals to Newcastle."

There was something special about Pamela, though. "Pam's natural innocence, brilliant smile and inner spirit caught my eye immediately and in person she was even lovelier than on film."

Grabowski rolled out the red carpet for Pamela, who had never even been on an airplane before. "They were wonderful people, they even gave Pam her own bodyguard," mom Carol remembered. As for her daughter posing nude, Carol was all for it. "I didn't have any qualms over Pamela appearing nude in Playboy. She's a beautiful girl, why not?" In fact, Pamela remembered her Mom saying that she herself would've done it had anyone asked her and that it would be something that Pamela would always have to remind her of her youthful beauty. Pam often quoted her mother's advice: "She said, 'Pamela, do it. If I had the body I would do it in a second.'"

The first shoot was in May 1989. It was for the October "Back to Campus" issue, an annual Playboy classic. Pamela was paired with photographer Stephen Wayda. She was given a red and navy school blazer with the Playboy bunny on a crest, a striped tie, a white shirt and a straw hat. The jacket, shirt and tie were artfully arranged to show the edge of Pamela's bare breast and the edge of her left nipple. The hat was used to cover her bare crotch. Even though the cover shot outfit revealed only a tiny portion of her assets, Pamela was freaked.

Behind the camera, Wayda only noticed one thing. "She was the quintessential college girl, with long straight sandy hair and cute figure, every college boy's dream. She had a look of innocence combined with a natural easy sensuality."

Then the waterworks started. That first day Pamela cried and cried. The photographers had to get the first cover shot out of only three rolls of film because of her tears. When the day was over, Pamela was a little angry, but mostly with herself. "I hated that I was so modest and insecure all my life. I thought, 'You know what? Nobody knows me here. I'm going to do it.' " Up until that day she had always considered herself a loner, but deep down inside she knew there was an extrovert waiting to bust out.

The second day Pamela was just fine. She said to herself, "This is a once in a lifetime opportunity. Just jump out of your skin and do it." She did better than that. She jumped out of her clothes and did a test shooting for a centerfold.

Still suffering from nerves, she giggled a lot, but everyone on the set knew that they were witnessing the birth of a modern-day Venus. Of course, it helped that Playboy had created a proper work environment. Nothing cold, or sleazy, just beautiful lingerie, luxurious bed linens, attentive hair and makeup artists and sensitive, encouraging people on the set. There were huge posters of beautiful women without their clothes everywhere Pamela looked and that helped, too. Before long, she even felt comfortable. "You get so used to not having clothes on that they have to stop you before you walk out on the street naked," she once wisecracked.

One year later, Pamela would say that it all boiled down to one thing. "When they asked me to come back to do a nude layout, I saw it as a business opportunity. My philosophy is that you only live once and you have to look at the whole process as a game. I go for it. If somebody's going to get a break, why not me?"

On the day of that historic original photo shoot, Pamela also dutifully filled out the Playmate Data

Sheet that accompanied her centerfold, which Playboy rushed into the February 1990 issue. Her entries revealed equal parts seriousness and silliness. Under "Turn-Ons" she wrote "Sincerity, honesty, strong arms, waffles and fried chicken." Under "Turn Offs," her responses were "Possessive men, jealous people, insensitive people & split ends." She admitted that her Valentine's Days plans were "Cooking a great dinner for a special man, wearing my sexy little French-maid outfit."

Pamela was totally shocked when she saw those first Playboy pictures. "I had no idea how beautiful they were going to look," she said. "I was really nervous because people are told that it's wrong and that you have to wear clothes, but after a while it became fun. I've always thought there was a barrier for me to cross, to be myself. And when I did Playboy for the first time, that was it. It was just like playing a character and it felt good that I could be that way instead of hiding. I've always been kind of modest but it was good because it really built my self-confidence."

And it also built her bank account. Pamela was paid $15,000 for that first layout, which was a lot more money than she'd ever made for one day's work as a model in Vancouver. Pamela felt taken care of by Hugh Hefner's organization and she was even invited to his mansion, where she met actors like James Caan and Tony Curtis. Playboy's Marilyn Grabowski in particular was extremely supportive and friendly. She took Pamela to dinner at the Hollywood hotspot Spago one night and told her that she had what it takes to be a celebrity and a star and all she had to do was put in the effort. Grabowski remembered that Pamela turned heads just walking through the restaurant. And when the women finished dinner and headed for home, the paparazzi, who were staked out at the restaurant waiting for celebrity arrivals and departures, took Pamela's picture — even though none of them knew who she was. Yet.

Pamela instinctively knew that she was in the right place at the right time and exactly where she was supposed to be. After all, she had written in her Playmate Data Sheet that "Being a Playmate means the start of something big." She took Grabowski's advice to heart.

She also took another piece of advice after doing that first Playboy layout. She kept hearing how this actress and that model had undergone breast enlargement surgery. "When I came to Los Angeles and started talking to all these people, I really got caught up in it. Almost everybody I met had breast implants." She heard it so much that she decided that it couldn't possibly hurt if she had implants, too. She went to talk to a plastic surgeon and within two weeks she had the operation, before, she admitted, "I had really thought it through. I felt that the pain and aggravation I went through wasn't worth it."

"Nature gave me 34-C boobs," she has said. "But I always felt like a sparrow chest, so I thought maybe if I had breast implants it would help my figure and give me the cleavage I wanted." Instead, the operation proved disappointing. She woke up thinking, "Is that all there is?" even though the operation had changed her bra size from a 34-C to a 36-D.

Having done what so many actresses before her had done, Pamela decided to stay put in Los Angeles and see what would happen if she tried to become an actress. She had already done some modeling for the sexy Frederick's of Hollywood catalog and she had a growing profile because of her appearances in Playboy. She declared that she'd go back to Vancouver when people stopped offering her work. That was simply not going to happen. Even so, the early days were lean. Pamela remembers packing up a $500 Honda with doors that had to be tied shut and moving to Newhall, a suburb north of L.A., "with a fork, a spoon and a plate." Later she got a TV.

That came in handy, for she was soon going on auditions for sitcoms. Casting directors may not have been aware of those early Playboy appearances, but they nevertheless found Pamela Anderson hard to resist. Although she had no formal training as an actress and no real experience either — in 1990 she made her TV debut on Married...With Children, a show that had made a star out of Christina Applegate and knew a good thing when they saw one.

And so did Tim Allen. The stand-up comic had the starring role in Home Improvement, playing a TV carpenter. Pamela was hired to play his sidekick, Lisa, the Tool Time Girl. For $1,500 a week she wore low slung overalls and smiled and had the same dialogue week after week: "Does everybody know what time it is?" she would ask. The answer, week in, week out, was an enthusiastic "Tool Time!" It came from the studio audience who flocked to see Home Improvement being filmed and from a growing number of Americans who would soon make the program the number-one show in America.

Only some of Pamela's new admirers knew her from the pages of Playboy. One was a veteran of a top TV show himself, one who had seen Pamela Anderson as a glossy centerfold and desperately wanted a date. His name — Scott Baio.

Chapter 5

SCOTT BAIO COULDN'T HAVE been more different than Pamela Anderson. He was born in Brooklyn, New York, in 1961, and had big city style and streetwise sophistication. Scott was a star by the time he was a teenager, appearing opposite the young Jodie Foster in a kiddie gangster film called Bugsy Malone. That role showed that he could play a tough guy and be a comedian and it brought Scott to Los Angeles, which led directly to the role that made him famous — playing Charles "Chachi" Arcola — on Happy Days.

"Chachi" was the younger version of the show's standout character, Fonzie. He had all the swagger of a Brando and all the sweet teen appeal of an Osmond. Baio played the role for eight seasons and went on to star in several sitcoms afterward. By 1991, he had started to direct television shows as his acting career began to slow down. One thing he hadn't lost, though, was his way with women. Baio was one of Hollywood's most desirable bachelors with a long string of conquests.

According to Pamela, he was also "the most unromantic guy in the world. On our first Valentine's Day, he gave me floor mats for my car and at Christmas, he gave me a sewing machine." Baio was apparently already thinking and acting like a suburban husband, not a Hollywood lover.

That might have been tolerable, if a little dull, but there was something else that bothered Pamela. She had begun to get the feeling that Scott wanted a wife and mother, not necessarily an independent 24-year-old woman who was motivated enough to pursue her own goals. By the end of the year, as Baio spoke more and more about marriage, Pamela knew that at this point in her life and career, such a union to Scott Baio would be "a disaster." Scott was still under the wing of his father, Mario, who was trying to boost his son's career and begun dictating that Pamela's career should take a back seat.

That was not about to happen. Pamela was scheduled for another Playboy cover and her role on Home Improvement was beginning to bring offers of other TV work, one of which would catapult Pamela into the stratosphere.

Baywatch: Panic at Malibu Pier had been filmed as a pilot for a new NBC show in 1989. It starred David Hasselhoff, a tall, blue-eyed hunk, who'd gotten female hearts pumping on The Young and The Restless for seven years before becoming a prime-time TV star on Knight Rider. In Baywatch, Hasselhoff played Mitch Buchannon, the leader of the guards at a fictional Los Angeles beach, who was so devoted to his job that his marriage had crumbled around him. The first episode was a success and the series was quickly picked up, then abruptly dropped after one season due to poor ratings.

Most actors would have started looking for the next job, but for Hasselhoff, who was as devoted to the show as his character was devoted to his lifesaving, it was merely a temporary setback. Hasselhoff took a deep breath and plugged on. The show continued, sold on a syndicated basis in which independent television stations across America bought the rights to broadcast the show to fit into their program schedule on a day and time of their choosing. It became a hit, offering equal opportunity ogling to both sexes. Hasselhoff was not only the star, he was now also an executive producer and stood to make a fortune selling the show around the world.

Pamela had been asked to try out for Baywatch before, but could never seem to make it down for an audition. "I was famous for not showing up, famous before I walked through the door." When she finally did, however, she was offered a job on the spot. Later, one of the producers told her it was because she didn't wear a bra to the audition. Pam recalled, "I didn't even think about that. I had a low-cut denim shirt on and I was like, 'Wow, I'm glad I overwhelmed you with my acting ability.'"

By the time Pamela arrived, the show had settled into a remarkably simple formula: A group of very good-looking, very fit male and female lifeguards patrolled the beaches looking for people in trouble. They ran into the surf with an orange flotation device under their arm, saved somebody and emerged from the water looking heroic and sexy. There were montages where they didn't even speak dialogue, just went about their business to the soundtrack of cheesy pop music. A lot of the scenes that Baywatch became famous for — and were subsequently spoofed — had a soft-core sensuality to them, women in second-skin red bathing suits, running across the sand in slow motion. People magazine called it a "super sexy amalgam of hormones and Coppertone." One of those rare television shows that capture the popular imagination without pretending to be anything other than popular entertainment, Baywatch was critic-proof.

Occasionally the hour-long episodes would involve the personal lives of the characters, as if anyone really cared, who were mostly noble, untroubled and uncomplicated people. Pamela played CJ Parker, who was a bit more interesting than most. She was a beach hippie, a sweet, sunshiny soul who gazed into crystals, wore a toe ring and sometimes braided her hair in the front. She was unmistakably the star of the show, even though it was created for David Hasselhoff, who eventually made millions since he owned a percentage.

CJ was a character that Hasselhoff and the writers had created after the show was already in full swing and they didn't know what they were going to do with her. Eventually, they tailored the character around Pamela, turning her into a saxophone player, as Pamela had been in her high school band, and giving her an interest in mystical things.

In 1992, Pamela became a split personality. Some days she was CJ parker on Baywatch. Other days, she was Lisa the Tool Time girl on Home Improvement. Neither required a great amount of acting talent, but it did mean a lot of running around. Pam had moved to a condo on the beach in Malibu, which made it a little easier, since Baywatch was mostly filmed in nearby Santa Monica.

She was single, but not for long. There was a guy on the set she had noticed, French-born actor David Charvet. "My first impression," Pam recalled, "was 'Wow! This guy is too good to be true.' He had looks, class and more charm than any man I had ever met." At the end of a day's filming, they would "cozy up and let the rest of the world go by." People who worked on Baywatch thought they were good together. "Pamela felt she had met her match — mentally and physically," said one fellow employee. They began living together almost instantly.

Charvet was five years younger and Pam enjoyed

playing the role of the sensual older woman. "He was very young and wet behind the ears," she said. "I taught him how to love. I created him as a lover. I showed him what I liked and what turned me on."

Charvet was equally smitten. He told friends that Pam gave him the space he needed and that he had no problem with her being America's favorite Playmate. "What Pam does for Playboy is her own business," he told friends. "That's fine with me."

Maybe it was, but Pamela noticed that he had a moody streak. She had also accepted a film role in a movie called Snapdragon. It required nudity and it was a tough shoot. Charvet didn't seem to be very supportive about her work on the film, but he was nevertheless still pressing for a more serious commitment that for whatever reasons, Pamela just didn't want to give. And by the time the summer of 1993 rolled around and Pamela had quit Home Improvement, the two of them were back on Baywatch. Not as lovers anymore, but merely as co-stars.

It was a tense time for Charvet, who admitted that Pamela was his first real love. So tense, in fact, that one day when Pamela flubbed her lines, David kicked sand in her direction. It was windy and the sand went in Pam's face. "It's really hard for me to work with her. Every time I look at her, I remember the good times," he told a pal.

Meanwhile, Scott Baio had been trying to win Pamela back all through the summer of 1993. He bombarded her with telephone calls, notes and daily floral arrangements. He took her out to romantic dinners. He proposed and they were officially engaged in September, but two weeks later, after spending the weekend in Seattle to promote Baywatch, she called him up and called it off. She told him that she had thought about it and just couldn't marry him. She then called a courier service and had the engagement ring sent back to Baio. Pamela didn't even want to see him, a friend recalled. Pam had realized that Scott hadn't changed much since they went out two years before. He seemed to have everything all planned out, and Pamela's career didn't figure into the equation. Pam felt like she was going to end up barefoot and pregnant, instead of continuing to bare all in Playboy and nurture her own career.

Scott, despite hoping that Pamela and he might reconcile, grew hurt and angry once the ring arrived. Still, he tried to win Pam back, but she would only speak to him a couple of times on the phone. It wouldn't be the first or the last time that Pamela would reunite with someone who still carried a torch for her and end up sending the poor guy down in flames.

Chapter 6

"I SUPPOSE I AGREED to marry Scott because I wanted some stability and companionship in my life," Pamela said, trying to her explain her impulsive behavior. "What I forgot was that it has to be the right person. I see now that getting engaged on the spur of the moment like that was a really silly thing to do. It certainly is not a way to find lasting happiness."

Later Pamela would come to realize that just because she wasn't an alcoholic like her father didn't mean that she didn't have an addictive personality. In fact, she admitted, "I have addictive traits in love and relationships. My family is in Canada, so sometimes I feel I have nobody here in L.A. So it's difficult sometimes and that's why I'm into relationships a lot — maybe looking for that comfort or love."

She did feel comfortable and loved when she was with David Charvet, so it came as no surprise that just a few weeks after she broke up with Scott Baio, Pamela and David started seeing each other again. Baywatch staff noticed that they visited each other's dressing rooms and slipped off to have quiet lunches alone. "Neither of us was angry when we broke up," Pamela explained.

But it didn't take long for Pamela to realize that they'd be much better off remaining friends. Just a week after it was reported that she and Charvet were an item all over again, Pam started dating another actor. His name was Dean Cain, a tall, dark and handsome former football player who had gone to Princeton, where he dated Brooke Shields. Pam spotted him at a party when she was engaged to Baio. After she called off the wedding, Pamela discovered that Cain was going to be the new Superman on the ABC TV show Lois & Clark. In late November 1993, she gave him a call.

This was a unique situation for Pamela; one of the first times she actively pursued a man. He took her out to dinner in Malibu and they then became pretty much inseparable. In Cain, Pamela seemed to have found the perfect man. He was college-educated and physically gifted. "Without his clothes on, Dean Cain has the greatest butt in the world," Pam told a girlfriend. "And that body. I just melt into his chest like butter. I want to spend the rest of my life with this guy."

The Princeton grad was also well-endowed. "Put it this way, there isn't a woman on earth who wouldn't be happy with what he's got," Pam told a friend. "The butt view is impressive but when the guy turns around, your eyes pop out."

The imaginative Cain liked to re-create erotic scenes from classic movies and they would frequently rent videos to spice up their lovemaking. One of their favorites was the scene in 9½ Weeks, where Mickey Rourke blindfolds Kim Basinger and gets freaky with her using the contents of the refrigerator. Another was the highly charged moment where Jack Nicholson has his way with Jessica Lange on a kitchen table in The Postman Always Rings Twice.

Cain might have been a hot-blooded stallion in bed, but when it came to commitment, he was a cold fish. He made it no secret to Pamela that he wasn't into having a serious long-term romance. Still, she went out of her way to plan picnics or arrange romantic dinners at expensive restaurants, only to be stood up by Cain. "Pam was always on the phone trying to track him down," a friend remembered. "She had no pride where he was concerned. She'd do anything."

Cain cruelly dumped Pamela after meeting model and professional beach volleyball player Gabrielle Reece. Cain called Pamela up and asked her to please stop calling him. Then, to add insult to injury, he started telling his friends that Pam simply wasn't his intellectual equal. "She's the most beautiful girl I've ever seen, but it just didn't work," he said. Naturally, the comment made its way to Pam, who was brokenhearted. She called him a creep at the time, but a year later, she had mellowed and simply said, "We all make mistakes. I had a physical relationship with Dean, but we're not friends now. He's not a lover I particularly want to think about."

She hardly needed to. By that time, Baywatch was an international sensation and Pamela Anderson was one of the few women in the world who could have any man she wanted. Though she was devastated by the way Dean Cain treated her, it didn't stop Pamela from looking for love. This time she was determined to find somebody whom she was attracted to both physically and emotionally.

Shortly after Dean dumped her, Pamela hooked up with Eric Nies, a cute and muscular model and actor who had shot to fame on MTV's Real World. Like Pamela, he had experienced sudden fame and they seemed to have a great deal in common. Pamela said Eric was "like my best friend — so we can just relax and be ourselves with each other." Eric had been such a striking and sexy presence on Real World that there was no question that he would become a star and soon landed a job with the music television channel, hosting the MTV after-school dance party called The Grind.

Their short affair turned out to be just that — a grind. In June 1994, Pamela decided to pay a surprise visit to her sweetie who was filming his show at Zuma Beach, California, which was within driving distance from Pamela's home in Malibu. But when she arrived at Nies' trailer she found a woman modeling a bikini for the hunky host. "What's going on?" Pam demanded, pushing the girl out of the trailer. After she departed witnesses heard the sounds of clattering and breaking objects. Pam stormed out; Eric went clubbing with his buddies that night.

They patched things up, but it was like trying to put a Band-Aid on a broken leg. Several weeks later, Eric was observed getting all snuggly with Pam's Baywatch co-star Nicole Eggert. The strange thing about that was that even though Nicole had said she was leaving the show because of all the attention that Pam got from her engagement to Scott Baio — who just happened to be Nicole's first love — Nicole initially helped fix up Pam and Eric. They had met one night at The Viper Room, Johnny Depp's rock 'n' roll hotspot. "He kept staring at me," Pam said. "We talked a little while as I was leaving and Eric got in touch with me through Nicole."

By the end of the summer, the Pam and Eric dance ground to a halt. He had taken Nicole to meet his parents. And true to her own admission that she was addicted to love, Pamela Anderson wasted no time finding a new man.

Single once again, Pamela traveled to the French resort of St. Tropez. The trip was notable in the transformation of Pamela Anderson, who was always happy to explore a new look. "What really sets Pamela apart," photographer Stephen Wayda said, "is that she has a very clear vision of where she wants to go. She wanted to break out of the confines of the backwaters of Vancouver and get everything she could out of life."

On Baywatch, she had braided her hair at the sides; in St. Tropez, her fifth shoot for Playboy, Pamela adopted a sultry look not unlike that of another famous Playmate — Brigitte Bardot. Working with the Playboy team, Pamela had tousled blond hair, full lips, dramatic eye makeup and arched brows. She had not quite achieved the blow-up sex doll look she would eventually adopt with fully lined lips and huge platinum hair, but she was well on her way. For most of the shoot she wore nothing but long strands of beaded jewels and shells. By this time, posing nude had become just like modeling swimsuits, she said — except that she didn't have to worry about how the swimsuit looked. One day, while scouting locations, she met a bronzed Adonis. It didn't take Pamela long to convince the Playboy photographer to photograph them together. Upon her return, she declared that St. Tropez was her favorite place in the world.

Later that summer, she started filming Baywatch again. Pam was "trying to focus on myself and my career." Again, she was not keeping company with a man, only with one of man's best friends. "I spend a lot of time with my golden retriever," she said. "These days my idea of a perfect evening is to put on some sloppy clothes and watch TV, curled up with the dog."

By September 1994, she'd found another dog, this one was of the two-legged variety. Like Star, her golden retriever, Bret Michaels had shaggy blond hair. He'd also been around the block a few times. As the lead singer for a hair metal band called Poison, who had enjoyed some success in the 1980s, Michaels was well known for his exploits with groupies. This didn't seem to bother Pam one bit. If she had learned one thing, however, it was that men might appreciate a girl who puts out, but they don't respect or want to marry a pushover.

With that in mind, Pamela kept Michaels waiting for 10 weeks before sealing the deal. After the first four weeks, an understandably frustrated Michaels, who was used to having his way with girls backstage and on his tour bus, told Pamela that he was accustomed to sleeping with girls on the first date (if not sooner).

"I was stunned," Pamela recalled. "I said, 'I need to get to know you better. If you don't respect me or like me for that, fine. But that's the way I am.'"

Michaels hung in there and a physical relationship developed. They "made love" Pamela said, instead of just having sex. "I need to be good friends with a man before I even consider going to bed with him. I don't want sex. I want men to make love to me. If I slept with all the guys I'm supposed to have slept with, I'd still be recovering."

It peeved Pam that "every time I go out with a guy, I'm supposed to be having wild crazy sex with him." And she was smart enough to know that that particular perception could be very dangerous — not just to her reputation, but to her safety.

That fall, she led a one-woman campaign to convince David Hasselhoff to hire a round-the-clock security guard for her. She had been stalked, she said, by a lot of people in the last few months and was scared for her life. She even moved into a hotel for several months while workers installed a high-tech security system in her Malibu home.

Pamela had already had a brush with creepy guys at work. "I walked off the beach once and saw a guy masturbating in his car while watching us do a scene," she recalled. She was not really sure that some fans knew where to draw the line and felt that her privacy was at stake. "There's a little scariness that comes along with it," she explained. "Like when I get a letter addressed Pamela Anderson, Movie Star and it's in my mailbox from Germany." And she had begun to receive even more disturbing letters. One really scary guy sent her naked pictures of himself and said he had wounds on him that he had named after Pamela.

In October 1994, Pamela visited Michaels in

New York, where she felt considerably safer. They went out on the town, keeping late hours at the hippest clubs in town. She was having a good time and her guard had been let down, so when she appeared on Howard Stern's radio talk show, Pam used the opportunity to blast Baywatch for not taking care of her. "I have one year left on my contract. But the only reason I would ever leave is if I didn't feel safe. It's not worth risking my life over. All I want is for someone to escort me home."

She said that Bret normally looked after her when he was in town, but he had been away on tour. During the interview, she also revealed that she had a way of comforting herself when her boyfriend was not around. She pulled out a photo of Bret that she kept in her purse, proudly displaying it to Stern. It wasn't a picture of Bret, but of "little Bret." If Pamela couldn't have her man with her at all times she was going to settle for having a picture of his manhood. People who saw it said Pam was in that photo, too, in a most uncompromising position. There would be more of these kinds of souvenirs, made on videotape, that would later come back to haunt Pamela, but at the time she didn't seem to care.

This was a new side of Pamela. She had always played around with her image as a sex goddess, saying that if people thought she was a dumb blonde, then she could only surprise them when they discovered that she could hold a conversation. "It doesn't bother me if some people perceive me as a bimbo. I see it as an advantage because then I have nothing to measure up to and I'll eventually prove them wrong."

Now, however, she seemed to be exhibiting a far less wholesome side of her sexuality. For a time, Pamela seemed to be as witty and wise about sex as Mae West and Marilyn Monroe. It was one thing to pose naked for photographs and to do nude scenes in erotic thrillers like Pam's straight-to-video clunker Snapdragon, in which she played a sexy serial killer with amnesia, but carrying around a picture of your boyfriend and yourself engaged in a sex act?

Fortunately, Howard Stern was just becoming a star and building his audience at the time and he hadn't penetrated the mainstream consciousness the way that Baywatch had. To most of the world, Pamela was just a pretty blonde who made grown men dream about mouth-to-mouth resuscitation. Most Baywatch fans had no idea that she had displayed photographic evidence of her other pulse-raising oral skills. Consequently, Pamela didn't really suffer a backlash as a result of her raunchy show-and-tell session on the radio show. It probably wouldn't have bothered her much, because at the time she believed that there was no such thing as bad publicity.

She was soon to learn otherwise.

Chapter 7

MEANWHILE, BACK AT THE beach, there was a small storm brewing on the set of Baywatch. A new actress, Yasmine Bleeth, had joined the cast, replacing Nicole Eggert and, like Nicole, Yasmine had already gone on a few dates with David Charvet. Pamela wasn't too happy about that, not because she didn't wish David well, but because it could turn into a Baywatch Love Triangle. Pamela thought she could handle things quietly, to set Yasmine straight about how these things might be interpreted by the press. What had been a few discreet words between two actresses in a dressing room, namely Pamela asking Yasmine something along the lines of keeping her personal and professional lives separate on the set, was soon reported as a bitter rivalry.

The worst, however, was yet to come. Pamela had pretty much moved into Bret's multimillion-dollar ranch home in Calabasas, California. One day that fall, when Pamela was at Bret's house, her legs gave out from under her. Pamela had fainted many times before, and she suffered from panic attacks, but Bret became worried and called an ambulance. Pamela was taken to the emergency room at West Hills Hospital where she was treated for exhaustion. She was certainly under a lot of stress and was working very long days on Baywatch, where it was written into her contract that she had to maintain her 112-pound figure. After she was released from the hospital, Pamela was ordered to get a few days of peace and quiet at home.

Things were tense on the set of Baywatch when she returned. Even though Pamela had cleared her name, David Hasselhoff was worried about how such stories could affect the popularity of his show. Baywatch had first become a hit in Europe and now that it was a sensation in America, Hasselhoff had big plans to turn the show into the world's guiltiest pleasure. He was not about to let it all sink because of a controversial actress, but there was just one problem: That actress happened to be the reason people watched the show. There was absolutely no question about it. Baywatch may have been making Hasselhoff a lot of money, but it had already made Pamela Anderson a star.

So even as Hasselhoff imposed strict contractual obligations on Pamela — she couldn't change her hair color and cut and could not have plastic surgery or tattoos without giving the producers 30 days notice — he was also planning to turn Baywatch into a global phenomenon.

Part of that plan involved filming special Baywatch movies, two hours worth of sun, sand and sex appeal. The first one, Forbidden Paradise, was shot on location in Hawaii in late 1994.

Pamela had a major role, one that required her to play love scenes with her former boyfriend, David Charvet. By then they had achieved a nice working relationship. "We've had our ups and downs but we're probably like brother and sister now," Pamela confessed.

The script called for David and Pamela to share a long, passionate kiss under the Waimea Falls in Oahu. Pam, who had recently been seen sporting a new engagement ring given to her by Bret Michaels, was certain this would not pose a problem for her. "Bret understands what I do for work and he's not jealous," she told friends. But Bret accompanied her to Hawaii and showed up on the day they filmed the makeout scene. At one point, after the director called cut, Pam and David exchanged a few words. When they took a break, Bret cornered Pamela and accused her of not acting — meaning he thought she was enjoying the kiss a little too much. According to observers, Pam shot back, "I don't tell you how to write your songs — if you can't handle the heat, stay out of the kitchen. I can't help it if you're insecure about our relationship."

Bret snapped back, telling her she was flaunting it in his face. After the next take, Pam and David continued kissing for at least half a minute, even though the director had called "Cut!" Again, Bret confronted Pamela on her next break. "You're too

much. I can't stand this bullshit," he screamed.
"Go mess with someone else's mind."

By the time the shoot was over and Pamela
returned to her room, Bret had left the hotel and the
island. It was the beginning of the end. "I can't
deal with it when men want to control my life,"
Pamela told friends. "I always get stuck with those
kind of boyfriends."

She was about to get unstuck. Pamela was headed
to Australia to host the Coca-Cola Surf Classic.
Bret was supposed to be joining her, but after his
immature behavior in Hawaii, Pam decided to go
alone. It was just as well. Bret and Pamela met when
they both became investors in a nightclub called
Sanctuary that had recently opened, so she assumed
that he would be looking after their best interests by
spending his evenings at the club. When she tried
phoning him, however, she could never reach him
there.

Pam already had her suspicions about Bret. He
was a reputed womanizer and when they met he
was still going out with another woman who was
so obsessed with him that she'd drive by his house
every day to see if he was with someone else.
When Pamela would visit, Bret would have her
Ford Bronco parked on the side of the house so the
woman who was checking up on him couldn't see
that he was entertaining. He'd had a weekend

rendezvous in Seattle with a stripper who worked in a Los Angeles club. She'd also heard rumors that he was up to no good when she was out of town.

So there Pamela was, thousands of miles away in Australia, having to deal with her uncertainties and trying to get her boyfriend on the phone. When she finally did reach him, she let him have it. "You haven't been to our club once since I've been away," she screamed. "I know what you've been doing with your nights. You've been with your bimbos. I know you're cheating on me!"

Bret was indignant. So what if he had? He told her when they met that no woman could own him.

"Then," said Pam, "Good riddance!"

"It was just too difficult to maintain the relationship," she told a reporter in Australia. "Some people find it hard to differentiate between what's for the camera and what's for real — but that's their problem. It's run its course and I'm very happy to be single again." It was something that Pamela always said when a romance went south, but she obviously was not very happy being single or why would she continue to throw herself into a new relationship within weeks of ending the previous one? There was a pattern developing: Each new love affair was more torrid than the one before and came to a bitter end even quicker than the one she had just gotten out of.

There were many possible explanations for these dramatic hit-and-run romances. Perhaps Pamela's success made it so difficult for the men she went out with that they became jealous of her fame? Maybe she really was addicted to love and got her kicks trying to tame bad boys? Perhaps these cads and carousers were the only guys that turned her on or the only ones she thought she deserved?

Looking back on the relationships she'd been in, there seemed to have been some improvement. She wasn't going out with guys who threw her out of moving cars or men who stood in the way of her career. And now that she was a star, perhaps Pamela Anderson had finally come to the realization that she didn't have to put up with liars and cheats.

There was a New Year on the horizon — 1995 — and after being dumped by Dean Cain and duped by Eric Nies and Bret Michaels, Pamela was more than ready for a change and had a few New Year's resolutions to make.

Chapter 8

"AT NIGHT I DREAM of living on a ranch in the middle of nowhere away from all the cameras. I'm with a nice ordinary guy who loves me and we're surrounded by my dogs, horses and babies."

Pamela Anderson had always dreamed of being a wife and mother. "I've been a full-blown mother since I was a little girl," she once said. "My brother Gerry is four years younger than me and I thought he was born for me. I looked after him like he was my own." Pam always imagined that she'd start having kids before she turned 20. "My cousins had kids when they were 16, 17, 18." Pam herself was the daughter of a teenage bride. "That's where I come from."

And look where she wound up. Sure, she was rich and famous and lived in a dream house in Malibu, not a shack in Comox, British Columbia, but she was also 27 and still single. She remembered what her grandmother said when Pamela turned 25. "You're a quarter of a century old and you're not married. Who's going to want you?" It was a joke, but it was also the truth. And the truth hurt. Plenty of men wanted Pamela, but not the way she wanted to be wanted. She was still a smalltown girl clinging to the dream of marriage and kids.

Sometimes it seemed to her that being Pamela Anderson was the only thing standing in the way of

Pamela Anderson's happiness. Her celebrity meant any hope for a normal life might never be in reach.

One thing Pamela decided was not to get involved in another hot and heavy romance right away. She had been impulsive in love before and it hadn't gotten her any closer to realizing her dreams of marriage and motherhood. She had been engaged four times, but always to men who wanted to own her. Some of them were cheaters, some of them brutes. None of them really accepted her for who she was — an independent woman who could make the separation between her sexy public image and her conventional ideas of private life. The men in her life either wanted her to give up her career and stay at home or to be the understanding sex symbol who didn't mind when her boyfriends strayed.

So Pamela decided to play the field a bit. When she was in Hawaii filming the Baywatch movie she got reacquainted with Kelly Slater, a professional surfer who had a guest role in some Baywatch episodes earlier that summer. Kelly had convinced her to host the Coca-Cola Surf Championships, in which he was competing, so he was there to lend a tanned shoulder for Pam to cry on when she finally ditched Bret Michaels.

Kelly was a real catch. He had been engaged to a beautiful model, Bree Pontorno, but broke it off when he realized that Pam might have felt the same attraction to him as he felt to her. At 22, he was a world-title holder and was fast becoming the first superstar of the surfing world. He had just signed a million-dollar endorsement deal with a manufacturer of surf clothing and was getting film scripts sent to his home. Kelly was a good-looking, clean-cut, straight-living kid from Florida who called people "sir" and "ma'am." The new couple hung out together in Australia, always acting as though they were just friends when there were photographers present, but getting lovey-dovey in private. They stayed there two weeks and were, according to sources, virtually inseparable.

But when Pamela got back to Los Angeles, she also went out on some dates with Arsenio Hall, who was still red-hot, even though his hit talk show had gone off the air. They partied at Sanctuary, the Beverly Hills club that Pam co-owned, where they were seen hanging out in a cozy booth, holding hands and slipping out the back door in the wee hours of the morning. They shopped together and went to Starbucks.

Pamela seemed determined to start 1995 on the right foot and playing the field seemed to be a good way to do that. She knew that if she wasn't obsessing about the man she was with at the moment, she'd have a better chance of actually meeting Mr. Right.

That resolve began when she decided to go to the

New Year's Eve party at Sanctuary. If she didn't have a good time, at least she'd be able to see whether her investment was going to pay off. If there was any night to tell if a club was going to work, New Year's Eve would be the one.

It would also be the one night that changed Pamela Anderson's destiny.

As the clock struck midnight and the champagne corks popped, instead of the usual New Year's kiss, a man covered in tattoos came up to Pamela, grabbed her and licked her on the face. Despite his forwardness, she thought it was a pretty cool gesture. She gave him her number.

Almost instantly, she regretted it. "I never had the taste for the rock 'n' roll man," Pamela once insisted. She'd heard that "Tommy Lee wanted to meet me for years." She'd also heard a lot about his reputation and his turbulent marriage to Heather Locklear. Having witnessed the rock 'n' roll lifestyle in her relationship with Bret Michaels, Pamela was convinced that Tommy Lee was part of the fast-lane party crowd in Hollywood, a crowd she didn't want to be a part of.

In the weeks that followed, Tommy called her "like crazy." She didn't call back. She was still seeing Arsenio Hall in January, though that seemed to be cooling down. Pamela was also spending time with Eric Nies. They had had their share of problems — he, too, had a wandering eye — and the relationship fell apart when his golden retriever, Jason, attacked her dog, Star. Pam told Eric that either his dog went for a permanent walk or she would. Strangely, Eric chose his best friend, Jason.

When he heard that Arsenio was on his way out, Eric showed up with flowers and without Jason, whom he told Pam he'd gotten rid of. They, too, made the scene at Sanctuary, but the rekindled romance failed to catch fire. Pamela also met a wrestler named Shawn Michaels (no relation to Bret), who was known as "The Heartbreak Kid," when she hosted a wrestling event in Tampa.

During that time, Pamela was living with another man — 49-year-old Jon Peters, a former playboy hairdresser who had served as the inspiration for the sexy character Warren Beatty played in the hit '70s movie Shampoo. Peters' celebrity clientele helped him make the leap from the salon to the biggest studios in Hollywood, where he produced such blockbusters as Batman and Rain Man. Well-known around town as a stud, he had been married three times and romanced some of the most glamorous women in Hollywood, including Barbra Streisand, Nicollette Sheridan and Leslie Ann Warren. Jon had met Pam, 22 years his junior, at a party for Playboy a few years before, but at the time he was involved with supermodel Vendela.

When they amicably parted ways, the Swedish beauty, who'd always admired Pamela, left Pam's phone number on Jon's answering machine as a parting present.

Jon immediately began wining and dining Pamela at some of the best spots in Los Angeles. The town was abuzz with news of their romance and envisioned Peters molding Pamela into the next Marilyn Monroe. Though she claimed it was platonic, Pamela enjoyed the attention and care and all the good advice that a powerful man like Peters had to offer. "All my other boyfriends were just that — boys," she said.

Pamela spent weekends at his place in Malibu and when both of their homes were undergoing renovation, Jon got a suite for her next to his own at the Hotel Bel-Air. They frequently ate in trendy restaurants like Drai's and the Buffalo Club or had room service dinners together at the Bel-Air, rising the next morning for an early swim or a jog.

Meanwhile, Tommy Lee kept ringing and Pamela kept dodging his calls. When he did manage to get her on the phone, she finally gave him his one, and potentially only, chance, "I told him, 'You have 24 hours to take me on a date. Then I will never see you again,' " she remembers.

But then she had second thoughts. Then third and fourth thoughts. She had a friend call him up and tell him the date was off. But Tommy Lee wouldn't listen, at least not to an intermediary.

So he called Pamela one last time, who was getting ready to go to Mexico. She had a photo shoot for Playboy scheduled in the resort town of Cancun. She thought that Kelly Slater was going to be able to join her. She told Tommy not to get any crazy ideas about showing up there.

But Tommy Lee was not the kind of guy to take no for an answer.

Chapter 9

TOMMY LEE WAS THE drummer for Motley Crue, one of the most successful heavy metal bands of the 1980s. They formed when Tommy was just barely old enough to drive and recorded their first platinum LP when Lee was 19.

According to his entry in the Motley Crue autobiography, The Dirt, Tommy Lee was born Oct. 3, 1962, in Athens, Greece. His father, David, was an army sergeant who proposed to a former Miss Greece, Vassilikki Papadimitriou, the first time he laid eyes on her. They married five days later. She spoke no English and he spoke no Greek, so they communicated by drawing pictures for each other. She had five miscarriages and a son who died shortly after birth before she stayed in bed for the entire nine months of her pregnancy with Tommy.

Shortly after Tommy's birth, they moved to Covina, a suburb of Los Angeles. Tommy's father worked for the Los Angeles County Road Department, fixing trucks and tractors. His mother, who had been a model in Greece, became a maid. Tommy started banging on pots and pans as a 3 year old, took accordion lessons and dance classes, then picked up the guitar before getting back to drums and playing in the high school band. His other passion, from a very early age, was girls.

"My fate was sealed with my first crush," he wrote in The Dirt. "I'd follow her around on my bicycle and spy in her window at night like a pint-size stalker."

By the time he met Pamela, Tommy Lee had enjoyed a world of sexual experience. He was a self-confessed "rock pig" who had been married to Heather Locklear, the luscious blond star of Dynasty and Melrose Place, from 1986 to 1993.

After their divorce in November 1994, he had taken up with a beauty named Bobbie Brown, who had won the Star Search spokesmodel competition 14 times. They got engaged in June 1994, before his divorce from Locklear had been finalized. Even though he was arrested by police after a violent breakup with Bobbie, Tommy came crawling back in January, just a few days after he had licked Pamela's face and gotten her number. Bobbie took him and his ring back, only to give him his final walking papers in the beginning of February.

Lonely and depressed, the rocker then turned to his ex-wife for comfort after Brown sent him packing. Tommy suggested that he and Heather should start up again. She, on the other hand, wanted nothing more to do with the rock wildman after their divorce and she suggested that he start seeking professional help.

It was then that Tommy Lee became truly obsessed with Pamela Anderson. He had already been married to one of the most beloved babes of the '80s and he set his sights on Pamela as his next conquest. He was going to show Heather and Bobbie and he was willing to do whatever it took to get Pamela to notice him.

Pamela was not in the mood. She was already juggling several suitors and her career was climbing to new heights. Baywatch was on hiatus and she was getting ready to do her first major motion picture, Barb Wire. Plus, she had another Playboy layout in the works and her fee for showing off her figure for the magazine had increased substantially — well into the six figures.

She had let Tommy know that under no uncertain terms was he even to consider coming to Cancun as he had suggested. He must have considered her "no" as a double-dog dare, because before she knew it, he was on a plane and had tracked her down at the hotel where she was staying.

The shoot was not going that well. The first day was a disaster, recalled Stephen Wayda. The beach was packed and there were high rises blocking the sunset. They had to find a more remote location to get the pictures that Playboy was paying everyone so much money for. That suited Pamela just fine, since Tommy was in town, barraging her with phone calls. Unbeknownst to her, however, he was also partying and hitting on women like a frat boy at a bachelor party. According to a pal of his, he whooped it up in sleazy nightclubs that featured steamy lingerie shows and bikini contests. He picked up the winner of the bathing suit competition and, on another evening out, took four young tourists back to his hotel room

Finally, after the last day of the Playboy shoot, Pamela gave in. "I figured, 'What could go wrong? We'd just go out to dinner and have a lot of fun.' "

They certainly did. It was the day after Valentine's Day, but for Tommy and Pamela, it was like time had suddenly come to a standstill. According to Tommy's recollection in The Dirt, they went to a popular tourist bar, Senor Frog's, and one thing led to another and they went back to her hotel. They went out every night afterward until a well-lubricated Tommy borrowed a silver ring from a friend, slipped it on Pam's finger and proposed. She was laughing and crying and screamed, "Yes!"

They celebrated that Wednesday night in Room 6211, the $600 Presidential suite at the Camino Real hotel, where Pamela had been put up for the Playboy shoot. It was as if they were the only people on the planet, Pam would later recall, like they were Adam and Eve. "From the moment Tommy and I met, we could not keep our hands off each other," she recalled. "It was instant, mindblowing animal attraction. The sparks were literally flying.

Making love to Tommy seemed like the most natural and perfect thing to do. I knew I was madly in love with him. Tommy satisfied me in a way no man has ever done before. We made love morning, noon and night and sometimes, morning, mid-morning, noon, afternoon, evening and midnight."

Just as she had done in St. Tropez, Pamela talked photographer Stephen Wayda into taking some shots of her with her new lover. Tommy didn't know what he was getting into when he walked into the hotel room and, from that moment on, Pamela took control. She stripped off his shirt and positioned him so they both looked perfect. "You could see that they were totally enamored with each other and even forgot I was there," said Wayda about the photographs, some of which did appear in Playboy. "I just did my thing and shot my fill, recording them crazy in love with each other until even I found it too hot to go on."

And the whirlwind courtship continued. On Thursday, they went to the Ritz-Carlton hotel. They couldn't get in until Tommy put on a dinner jacket provided by the management over his jeans and tank top. The following night, they returned to the club La Boom with a gang of friends, where the group emptied more than a dozen bottles of Cristal champagne. Tommy drank cucarachas, a flaming drink made with Kahlua and tequila that he kept spilling, setting the table on fire. On Saturday they hit La Boom again.

On Sunday, February 19, they rested — but Tommy had one more event in mind. This time it was a surprise party and there was a man in a white suit in attendance. His name was Pedro Solis and he carried a briefcase. Pamela kicked off her black high-top sneakers and took a seat on a sun lounger next to Tommy. She was wearing a white bikini, around her waist there was a strip of fabric — something blue. Tommy was in knee-length denim shorts, naked to the waist, the word "MAYHEM" tattooed across his belly. They got comfortable on the loungers and sipped tropical cocktails called chi-chis.

The man in the white suit stepped forward, a sheath of papers in his hand. "Dearly beloved," he began in broken English. Within minutes, they had become man and wife. They rose to sign some paperwork and then toasted each other with plastic cups of champagne.

"I was sunning myself when there was a bit of a commotion by the place where they rent the diving gear," one member of a group of American students who witnessed the impromptu ceremony related. "I went over and there was Pamela Anderson in a tiny white bikini, sitting down getting married!"

"We cheered and clapped," said another witness. And, in return, the new Mr. and Mrs. Lee took a souvenir wedding photo with their fans, then proceeded to the water's edge where the registrar offered them congratulations and wished them good luck. With that, Tommy Lee swept his new wife off her feet — this time literally — and walked her into the turquoise waters of the Atlantic. As she squealed with delight, her groom gently tossed her into the waves.

"Tommy threw Pam into the water, which made the top of her bikini fly up," recalled the thrilled witness. "We all got an eyeful of everything!"

Soon afterward, Pam gushed to a girlfriend about the wedding: "I've thrown caution to the wind and I'm loving every minute of it. Tommy isn't just the life of the party. He is the party. Now he's my tattooed lover boy and I've never been happier."

Later, she would remark somewhat prophetically, "I didn't stop to think. Feelings like I had for him happen once in a lifetime. I knew if I ever did get married it would be spontaneous and romantic and this was beyond my wildest dreams."

Chapter 10

WHAT WAS BEYOND PAMELA'S wildest dreams was her mother's worst nightmare. "We never thought she would run off," Carol Anderson said, shortly after hearing of Pamela's spur-of-the moment wedding. "She just called and told me that she married that skinny tattooed kid who was married to that other woman on TV! We have no idea who this guy is. We've never met him. Pam never even mentioned his name to us before."

"I wish I'd tape-recorded everybody's reaction when we called to tell them. My best friend cried," Pam recalled. "My mother threw the phone."

Like most newlyweds, the Lees went on a honeymoon, a video camera packed among their other essentials. But unlike most newlyweds, their home movies turned out to be very revealing. And when this amateur-porn production popped up a year later on the Internet, and then in local video stores across America, it proved to be embarrassing and, even more, to become the stuff of legend.

After Tommy and Pammy returned home to Los Angeles, they continued to celebrate their love in unconventional ways. They decided to forgo the stuffy, traditional wedding bands and instead went to Sunset Tattoo in Los Angeles and spent a happy hour having each other's name inked onto their wedding ring fingers. His said "Pamela's"; hers, "Tommy's." For Pamela, diamonds were ridiculous. "I think diamonds have a relationship to your man's penis size," she proclaimed, meaning that the bigger the rock the smaller his c**k. Pamela had no complaints in that department. Tommy Lee had earned the nickname "T-Bone" for his hefty appendage, on which he also tattooed his wife's name.

The first week of their marriage was delirious. There was the quickie wedding, the sex-soaked postnuptial vacation and a reception in Los Angeles at Sanctuary where Pamela wore a silver-blue latex dress and the groom wore black leather pants and a white T-shirt. But by the 10th day, the honeymoon period was beginning to look like it was over. Observers at a Beverly Hills party noticed that when Pamela went to the bar, she saw her hubby getting chummy with another blonde. According to the report, Pamela screamed, "Hey, Tommy, your wife is over here!" Three nights later, at an L.A. club, it was Pam who had the attention of another man. An admirer ran his fingers through her hair and told her she looked beautiful. Tommy shoved the interloper and got socked in the kisser, but the other guy got bounced.

There was never any hope that Pamela and Tommy might settle down into happily-ever-after domestic bliss. She was now the reigning sex goddess of the 20th century and he was the most raunchy rock star the world had ever seen. Together, they were tabloid manna from heaven. Wherever they went, they could be counted on to be carrying on, whether they were carried away with passion or heatedly arguing. Not since Elizabeth Taylor and Richard Burton had a couple been so fond of fighting and making up. And they were kinky. One night, at a Lakers game, they had a tiff after Pamela showed off a tattoo to a group of male fans. The couple had a dust-up, then a makeup and a makeout session that was so erotic that they had to make an emergency stop at a piercing parlor called the Gauntlet in West Hollywood because Pam had bitten off Tommy's nipple ring in the heat of the moment.

Tommy was jealous and possessive, a compulsive flirt with a short fuse. He made headlines when he defended his right to privacy by threatening a TV crew with a shotgun outside the couple's Malibu home. Now that he was Mr. Anderson, he was constantly under siege, battling with photographers who wanted to get a picture of the hottest couple in Celebrityville. He also hated seeing pictures of his wife with anyone other than him. After ducking a photographer at the Expo club in New York, Pam and Tommy were granted sanctuary in the club's office, where he spied a photo of Pamela and her last love, Bret Michaels. "The only picture you should have on your wall is of Pam with me," Tommy shouted, after smashing his fist through the glass of the framed photograph.

Reports of these antics had begun to make their way back to David Hasselhoff, who was getting ready to shoot the next season of Baywatch. By then the show had become a tidal wave in the history of television. It was estimated that 20 percent of the world's population tuned in to get turned on by Baywatch. The show now had more than 1 billion viewers. When Communist China decided to let their people view Western television, the first show they broadcast was the surf opera watched in 142 other countries.

Although the program seemed to be little more than a jiggle-fest, Hasselhoff was drawing a huge paycheck by promoting it as a show steeped in family values. And he was certainly not about to let anyone — even the show's primary asset — upset his apple cart. Hasselhoff thought Pamela's bikini wedding gown was the height of bad taste and that her tattooed ring finger violated the clause in her contract about not changing her appearance without approval. There were rumors that he was so furious that he had started secretly auditioning actresses to replace Pamela and was having the script department figure out ways to bring her character to a tragic end. When he discovered that

Tommy had been calling Baywatch executives and campaigning for rewrites to make Pam's character more prominent in the coming season, Hasselhoff went ballistic.

"Pam's no longer the Barbie doll we all used to know and love," Hasselhoff was said to have told the Baywatch brass.

"What I do on my own time with my husband is my business," Pamela countered to a pal.

The problem was that Pamela was making it everyone's business. Where she had once raved about the physical passion they enjoyed in more general terms, Pamela was now sharing specifics. Like how they made love in the back of limousines and how she and Tommy had become members of the "mile-high club" by having sex in the bathroom of an airplane. There was even a rumor circulating that skin magazines like Hustler and the French edition of Penthouse had found explicit Polaroids of the Lees engaged in various sex acts. Asked about this, Pamela replied that they had been stolen from her home in Malibu and only expressed regret that she had made them available to someone with sticky fingers. "When I saw the first Polaroid," she commented, "I said, 'Whoa, baby! We should frame this.' "

While all of this infuriated Hasselhoff, it delighted the producers of Barb Wire, which was to be

Pamela's first major motion picture, a sexy sci-fi fantasy based on a comic book about a female bounty hunter. Of course, Pamela had appeared in some TV films and straight-to-video releases like Raw Justice, but this movie, backed by a major entertainment conglomerate, was going to be different. When Pamela first heard they were making a movie out of the comic book Barb Wire, which featured a female freedom fighter in a post-apocalyptic world — sort of a Mad Maxine — she was intrigued. Her agent at the time said. "No way." Pam said, "Are you kidding?" It was totally her, she thought. The first script she saw was campy and fun. She played this girl on a motorcycle with big hair and tight leather clothes who really kicked ass. The film was a dark comedy and supposed to be very much like a cartoon in the vein of Batman.

She signed on. Before a single foot of film was shot, Pam headed off to the Cannes Film Festival in the early summer of 1995. Cannes is notorious for publicity stunts. Brigitte Bardot and Sharon Stone both became international celebrities by working the press there. Each year, film producers and starlets do their damnedest to get their pictures taken, their movies talked about and their careers launched. For Pamela, making a big splash at Cannes was a no-brainer.

Pam was already a huge star in France and

throughout Europe thanks to Baywatch. Now, Richard Branson, the financial wizard behind the Virgin record label and airline, was experimenting with the idea of Pamela as a product, launching Virgin Cola in a curvaceously female shaped bottle called "The Pammy."

Needless to say, Pam's arrival in Cannes was eagerly anticipated. Plus, she had that good-looking, rebellious heavy metal musician husband with her. One day, during this promotional visit, Pamela and Tommy boarded a boat that brought them to a dock in the center of all the hustle and bustle of the festival. Other boats, filled with fans and photographers, were running into each other straining to get near. "Photographers were falling into the water," Pamela remembered. "Tommy was like, 'Wow, you are cool!'"

By the end of their stay at Cannes, Pamela and Tommy had gotten so much attention that the studio backing Barb Wire started to feel invincible. According to Pam, they tried to make the script that much more commercial. They added a lot of action sequences; they replaced the director with a man named David Hogan, whose previous experience was shooting rock videos for the likes of Sheryl Crow. Pam was starting to feel iffy about the whole thing, but she was under contract. "I wound up going against my instincts," she later recalled. "It was really difficult for me."

The premise of Barb Wire was pretty absurd: Barbara Kopetski was a bounty hunter who lived in a mythical place called Steel Harbor, which is a junkyard of corruption and civil war, "the under-belly of civilization," as Pamela described it. As a fierce woman who explodes if anyone calls her "babe," the impetuous Kopetski earns the nick-name "Barb Wire" for her tough exterior and a tat-too of barbed wire around her left bicep for which Pamela actually underwent the needle. As tough as she is, however, she was also a woman — one who wore heavy makeup, gravity-defying leather vests and took bubble baths with a loaded gun.

A freedom fighter during the recent civil wars in Steel Harbor, Barb has lethal skills she learned in the Army, but when the man she loves ditches her, she gives up the cause, isolating herself in a hatred for all men. All men, that is, except her brother, who is blind. Then, of course, the man she thought was gone forever, the man who causes her to become this violent loner, suddenly returns, asking Barb for a favor. "And," Pamela would explain, "we get through the whole thing and I save the world."

The work was long and grueling. There were big action scenes to choreograph, firearms to shoot and explosions that had to be set up before they could be set off. That meant that there was a lot of time that Pam would have to spend waiting for a scene to be set up. She killed time productively, entertaining her husband in her trailer where they were working on a production of their own: a baby. Tommy was always ready, willing and able to perform action sequences from his own imagination in the cozy confines of Pamela's double-wide. Rumors began to circulate that he would lock her in the trailer, demanding sex and holding up the production. Later, when the film was finished, Pamela would talk about those intimate moments — "Of course, Tommy and I had sex in the trailer on the movie set all the time, but that was both of our choices" — to any interviewer willing to listen. Not surprisingly, they all were.

Pamela also gave her all at work. Especially when it came to the stunts. "You've got to deliver your line while doing a couple of back flips and killing all the bad guys," she told a reporter. Pam "wanted this girl to exude sexuality even when she's fighting," so she did a lot of the fight scenes herself. It wasn't particularly easy, either. She had a corset that cinched her waist down to 17 inches and wore stiletto heels. She even did a fight scene 120 feet above ground, although she's mortally afraid of heights.

There was another much more frightening occurrence on Barb Wire. In early June 1995, Pamela collapsed on the set and was rushed to the hospital. She was having horrible stomach pains that she attributed to the tight leather corset she wore while doing stunts for Barb Wire. The doctor had good news and bad news. The bad news was that she had a burst ovarian cyst that required an emergency operation.

What was the good news?

Pamela Anderson Lee was pregnant.

Chapter 11

FINALLY, ALL OF HER dreams seemed to be coming true. Pamela Anderson was already a TV star, about to become a movie star and now she would be a mom. Just to be sure, she did a home pregnancy test on Father's Day and that, too, came up positive. The excited parents-to-be phoned everyone they knew. The first call went to Tommy's folks. Tommy had always wanted kids and claimed his ex-wife, Heather Locklear, wasn't ready. Pam went through her kitchen, junking any food that wasn't healthy, getting rid of $200 bottles of champagne. She had also given the producers of Baywatch an ultimatum. Having already gotten infections from swimming in the polluted waters of Santa Monica Bay, Pam told them she would be doing her Baywatching from the sand.

Having a baby on board did little to calm the waters of the tempestuous Lee marriage. The X-rated Polaroids did get in a sleazy sex paper called Screw and Pamela's friends blamed Tommy. The same day the magazine made its way around the set of Barb Wire, Pamela filmed a love scene with her co-star that was so heated her husband nearly threw a fit. Tommy complained to the producer so loudly that he had to be removed from the set.

Not long after that incident, on June 28, Pamela was on her way to work on Barb Wire, when she suddenly doubled over in searing pain. Her terrified husband bundled her into his Chevy Suburban and raced off to Cedars-Sinai Medical Center. In the emergency room, the doctors quickly feared the worst. Pam was checked into Room 8013 under the name of Pamela Bass and her personal obstetrician, Dr. Theodoric Hendrix, was paged.

Hendrix gave the distraught couple the news they feared the most. Still in her first trimester, Pam was having a miscarriage. She would also need to have a D & C to clear her uterus. The operation took an hour and Pamela was released the next day. Despite the disappointment, the couple was encouraged that she would probably be able to get pregnant again.

Three days later, Pamela turned 28. They had canceled a scheduled birthday bash and she was feeling blue. Tommy surprised her with gifts, including a $10,000 skull head ring studded with diamonds and sapphires and a matching necklace that he designed especially for her. Then he blindfolded her and drove his wife to the harbor at nearby Marina del Rey. When he removed the blindfold, Pamela blinked and let out an appreciative gasp. In the water in front of them was a 42-foot luxury yacht stocked with champagne, caviar, flowers and pink and purple balloons. They set sail on July 1, Pamela's birthday, and spent the

4th of July weekend on the boat and at the nearby Ritz-Carlton hotel.

The surprise voyage did the trick. "At first I didn't think I'd ever stop crying," Pamela remembered. "My heart is broken. I want a baby more than anything. I was just getting used to the idea of becoming a mom when the miscarriage happened. Losing the baby was tragic, but Tommy and I are now more determined than ever to have a child."

It didn't take the sexual Energizer Bunnies long. In August, Pamela announced she was pregnant again (it turned out to be wishful thinking), even as a cloud of controversy — allegations that Tommy was using drugs and beating his wife — began to appear on the horizon. There were also stories about his arrest for possession of a semiautomatic weapon, his past heroin use, and how he nearly died from an overdose a few months before his marriage.

Pam stood by her man, saying all those stories about his past were wrong. And she flatly denied that Tommy manhandled her. "It's ridiculous," she said. "Tommy is the most loving, caring gentleman I know. There's no way I'd stay with him if it was any other way." There were other rumors, too. That the couple was headed for divorce court and that she was being booted from Baywatch. Instead, Pamela said that it was she who was leaving the show to concentrate on her new film career.

She may have had high hopes for making the leap from the boob-tube to the big screen, but Pamela wasn't earning a reputation for professionalism on the set. Barb Wire began filming in late May with a 42-day schedule. Pam's ovarian cyst and miscarriage put the movie behind, and she missed 10 days of filming even when she was healthy. And her husband's presence on the set proved anything but helpful. "Whenever Tommy came to the set, Pam would run to her trailer for a sex break," an insider related. Once when a producer dared to interrupt their baby-making session, Tommy bellowed through the closed door of her trailer, "She'll be out when she's ready. She's the star of this damned movie."

Friends feared that Tommy was exerting a dangerous amount of control over his wife and sending her career down the toilet. Under his influence, she fired her manager, Ray Manzella, who had made both her and Vanna White household names, and he kept her out late at night, the reason for so many of her missed days on the set of Baywatch.

Pam knew what was happening but felt powerless, fearing she'd lose her husband if she didn't play along. "I knew my husband was a nonstop party animal when I met him, but I thought I could keep up with him. I've found out the hard way that I can't," she told a friend. It had a disastrous effect on her work habits. Pam called in sick so often that she had to be written out of several episodes for the 1996 season of Baywatch and the producers began to refer to Mondays as "No Pam Days." David Hasselhoff, who once adored her, now barely spoke to her. "I can't work and keep up with his partying at the same time," said Pam. "But if I want to hold on to him, I have to keep going as long as I can."

By October, the strain was starting to show. After attending a World Wrestling Federation event where she heard someone comment that her butt was big, Pamela went on a crash diet and became so scrawny that people feared she was suffering from anorexia. It was estimated that she lost between 10 and 15 pounds in six weeks on a diet of salad, rice, chicken, turkey and champagne. When David Hasselhoff ordered her to put the weight back on, Pam reportedly snapped, "You can never be too rich or too thin."

Apparently, her skinny-as-a-rail rocker husband agreed. Even as he was pushing his wife to the brink with his incessant demands for attention, he was also putting pressure on her to bring home the bacon. Since his band, Motley Crue, had split up before he even met her, Pamela was the main breadwinner in the family. All she wanted to do was put some money aside from all her hard work so that she could have his children and quit work to raise them. And all he wanted was for her to carry on.

He was good at carrying on. Pamela had never met anyone who partied as hard as Tommy and even though it was making her exhausted and emotional, she did her best to keep her man happy. On Oct. 3, 1995, Tommy turned 33. Pamela threw an outlandish bash. She hired performers from Cirque du Soleil, who painted their bodies silver. There was a lion and tiger that people could have their pictures taken with. She sent a tour bus to pick up the guests, rented a Ferris wheel and had a pile of junk turned into a giant drum kit for Tommy to play. She hired "little people" to say "Welcome to Tommyland" to the arrivals as they walked down a red carpet. She got a robe and a crown made of crystals made for her king and she dressed up as a ringmaster in shorts and fishnet stockings, carrying a whip. Pamela got the whole thing on videotape. "It looked like a Fellini movie," she said.

All the effort, however, did little to improve Pamela and Tommy's tempestuous relationship. Despite the birthday party, which had cost hundreds of thousands of dollars, they were just not getting along.

Tommy and Pamela were both still depressed over her miscarriage and they were bickering over just about everything. Then, on Oct. 12, 1995, Tommy started an argument with Pamela in her trailer on the set of Baywatch. It quickly spun out of control, with him screaming and busting up furniture. When he stormed out, he broke off the door to her trailer. Convinced that Tommy had finally left her, Pamela went back to their home.

Tommy came home later, wasted after a drinking binge with buddies. By then, Tommy recalled in The Dirt, they had already seen TV news coverage of video store shelves being stocked with their "honeymoon tape," so things were more tense than usual.

According to reports, he accused her of having an affair with David Charvet, her former Baywatch boyfriend. She tried to calm him, explaining that she and Charvet had filmed their last scene together a month earlier as he was leaving the show, but Tommy kept at it, getting more and more abusive and threatening. Now it was Pamela who was ready to walk.

She told him she was leaving and taking half her stuff with her. He pulled out a pistol and shoved it in her face, then pinned her up against the wall and pointed it at her neck. Pam fled, crying. She hopped in her car and drove to the condo she still owned in Malibu.

The following morning, Pam was a no-show on the Baywatch set. Nervous executives dispatched her bodyguard to pick her up. When he arrived at the Malibu condo, Pam was in a terrible state. She was naked, lying down by the door, complaining of dizziness, her body limp. Gasping for air and in obvious pain, she told her driver in slurred speech that she had taken too many pills and drank too much. "Call 911 right away," she pleaded.

Paramedics arrived at 7:45 a.m. They found an empty bottle of pills and a broken liquor bottle in the bedroom. Pamela said she'd drunk champagne and white wine and taken a sleeping pill. Since she could not stand, she was strapped to a gurney, covered with a blanket and whisked away to a nearby medical center where she was stabilized in the ER. She was then moved to Saint John's in Santa Monica for tests. Tommy arrived with red roses.

Soon they had the test results. Pamela had taken an excess of aspirin mixed with alcohol.

And she was pregnant again.

Chapter 12

AFTER HER MISCARRIAGE IN June, Pam was willing to take every precaution to make sure she carried her baby full term. She stopped partying and started eating. But she was still struggling with the top brass at Baywatch. Filming had to be delayed due to her movie commitment and hospitalization and everyone was on edge. One day, still exhausted, she took a nap in her trailer, keeping everyone waiting; another day she simply took off halfway through the day. When the producer chewed her out, Tommy left a threat on his answering machine. "If you make my wife cry again, I'll kill you," he seethed.

By the time they finally wrapped the season, everyone was glad it was over. The executives at Baywatch were hatching a secret plot to replace Pamela with newcomer Gena Lee Nolin if she or Tommy started causing trouble again. But Pamela wasn't even thinking about her hit TV show. Pam was in seventh heaven in her first trimester of Baby Watch. "I didn't give a second thought as to whether having a baby would harm my career," she said.

Her hormones had kicked in and she was feeling sexier than ever. "Carrying a baby made me feel like a real woman," Pamela announced. "I wasn't a little girl anymore." In an interview, she confided that she had had a swing installed in the living room ceiling of the couple's Malibu mansion. Tommy bought it for her. "He will sit at the piano and play music and I swing from one end of the room to the other — naked."

"Well," she added, "Sometimes with a big hat on."

They also renewed their wedding vows dressed in silver space suits. At their beach house, Pam played Malibu Barbie, trying on different outfits to amuse and arouse her husband. "If Tommy's in a bad mood," she revealed, "That's when I go upstairs and come down wearing this three-foot high Mad Hatter hat and high heels. He looks at me and cracks up — because that's all I've got on."

Pamela spent a fortune on lingerie and some-times she would convince him and one of his pals to put on a show for her. "I'll get them wearing my rubber dresses. I had them kick boxing in my bikinis once."

With the impending arrival of their first baby, everything seemed to be rosy. Pamela even got a $10,000-per-episode raise for the next season of Baywatch. By spring, she had almost convinced the world and herself that Tommy was just a big pussycat, who cooked and cleaned house for his wife now that she was in the family way. "I don't want to ruin his image, but Tommy is not what you think," Pam said. "He loves flowers. He knows the name of every plant and tree on the planet."

Pamela even put a spin on all the reports that Tommy had her on a leash so short and tight that it amounted to a choke collar. "What we're talking about is not being controlling, it's being crazy in love with each other. It's not that he doesn't trust me when I am away from him — he just doesn't want to be apart." She went on to say, perhaps trying to convince herself as well, that he would be a great father. "Kids love Tommy. With all his tattoos he's like a big coloring book and when he's in the swimming pool, kids try to rub them off. He loves it. Tommy's really like a little boy himself."

And boys will be boys. Tommy would do the shopping and cooking, but he would also get powerfully bored. He'd bring home kegs of beer and throw rocks at photographers trying to get a glimpse of preggers Pam. One day he and the missus got so stir-crazy that they hopped into his Ferrari Testarossa and zipped around the canyons of Malibu. When they found out their first child was going to be a boy, they chose the name Brandon Thomas Lee to honor Bruce Lee's son, who was accidentally killed while making a martial arts movie in 1993. Hoping that his son might follow in his own footsteps, Tommy even bought a drum kit for Junior, painted black with purple flames.

For the most part, things were relatively peaceful. "People think we have this really crazy rock 'n' roll lifestyle," said Pam. "But we wake up at seven and go to the gym every morning together." She was happy with the results; it seemed to balance out the well-endowed rocker. "Tommy got lucky being this skinny guy. But he's gained 30 pounds since I met him. He's finally got a booty. Now he looks all even, not like he's going to fall over when he's naked." She went on to say that her normally high sex drive had "gone through the roof" and seemed to indicate that she was getting plenty of relief in that department.

The first half of 1996 should've been the happiest time of her life. Pamela Anderson was finally pregnant and it looked like she was going to carry this baby to full term. To the outside world, she looked the way every first-time expectant mother should: radiant and filled with joy. Her little belly was swelling, as were her breasts, but it took quite some time before she started to show. In fact, she did a nude pictorial for Playboy when she was nearly four months along and continued to work on Baywatch, where she would be filmed behind towels and surfboards. At seven months, she did an ad for Coor's Light and a series of magazine covers to promote Barb Wire, which was finally due out early that summer.

On the set of Barb Wire, Pamela told an interviewer that she didn't care if she never made a movie again. (To date, she hasn't.) "The career that I want is motherhood," she declared. After the heartbreaking miscarriages she suffered, she was giddy by the time she reached her third trimester. She confided in an interview with Details that her plans were to breast-feed her child and revealed that she had taken a bath and noticed milk "squirting out of my breasts." In her joy, she left no details unmentioned. She talked about her ultrasound and how the doctor pointed out her son's penis. "I was very impressed," she said, "for a 7-month-old." Pamela seemed to be her old saucy self.

Later, however, Pamela would admit that her first pregnancy was a time of extreme mood swings and mixed emotions. On the one hand, she was thrilled that she was going to be a mom; on the other hand, she was dealing with her husband's childish behavior. Her life was a constant seesaw between the happiness and fulfillment of becoming a mother and the anger of having to deal with a husband who had suddenly witnessed his sex symbol wife turn into a very different person. Tommy grew cold and sometimes cruel. All was not well at the Lee household and though she constantly denied the fact that she and Tommy fought, the truth is they often did. "Being pregnant while in an abusive relationship," she told Jane magazine in 2002, "I was walking on eggshells, scared to be in the relationship, but too scared to get out. I felt so alone."

During the seventh month of her pregnancy, she shared a dream with the readers of Details. Pamela takes great stock in her dreams ever since her grandfather encouraged her to keep a journal of them. The dream, as she recalled it, was this:

"I dreamed that Tommy was taking me to Ronald Reagan's birthday party. We're all dressed up and pack all the baby things into the truck. When we get there we get everything out of the truck and there's Ronald Reagan and then there's four rows of kids, like four by four. There's a poodle in every row spaced between the kids on the diagonal. And they were all line-dancing. I'm sitting there watching the entertainment and Tommy goes, 'I'll be right back, I'm gonna go find a girl that looks like you.' So he leaves. I zoom in on Ronald Reagan and realize it's an impersonator. Oh, my God, he's left me in a mental institution with all my baby stuff. So I go running outside and I see four rows of women naked from the waist down praying to Buddha. I go, 'Excuse me, is there any way I can get a cab here?' And they go, 'Well, the men's cabs go to the right and the women's to the left and there's no cabs going to the left, so I think women can't get a cab today.' So I go inside and there's Anna Nicole Smith on an IV. I go, 'Do you need me to break you out of here?' And she goes, 'I can't. I'm a ward of the state.' So I'm like, 'Oh, my God, I really am in a mental institution.' I go outside again and I see this really tiny Lego car coming up to me. I'm trying to open the door really carefully cause I don't want to break it and my stomach's way too big. I look inside and there's Tommy in the front and he goes, 'I'm gonna break you out of here! Ya know what, I didn't really want to find a girl that looks like you. I just wanted to go party with my friends for a while — come on, get in.' And then I woke up."

A dream analyst came up with this explanation: "Beneath this dreamer's creative tapestry of surrealistic episodes is a reasonably coherent story about the inner concerns and fears (dependency, insecurity, abandonment, confinement) of a woman expecting a child. If much of this seems obvious, the dream is nevertheless riddled with enigmatic symbols, many of which suggest a very creative and humorous spirit."

The analyst did not know he was talking about Pamela Anderson, who was soon to become the sexiest mother in the world.

After her most recent miscarriage, which made news all over the world, Pamela decided that she didn't want to have her child in a hospital. She didn't feel comfortable there and was worried that photographers might be hiding out in the bathroom, dressing up as interns, trying to get pictures at the most private and vulnerable time of her life. She didn't want the experience to be spoiled. She had read a book called Birth Without Violence and talked to friends, one of whom had used a midwife. That's when she realized, people have babies everywhere — in taxis, in fields — so why shouldn't she have hers at home?

As she does with everything she sets her mind to, Pamela was determined to give birth in this very natural way. She thought it would be much more soothing and loving for the baby to be born at home instead of a brightly lit hospital. When the time came, around 9 a.m. on June 4, she had the tub in the bedroom of her Malibu house filled with warm water and spent most of the 17-and-a-half hours of labor in the bath. It became something like a ceremony, with candles burning and the hypnotic music of the group Enigma playing softly on the stereo. There would be no painkillers for Pamela, although Tommy had a headache and popped some Tylenol.

Toward the end, Pamela crawled out of the bath and was too scared to go back in the tub, so she delivered Brandon Thomas Lee, 7 pounds, 7 ounces, on the floor of her bathroom at 3:02 a.m. June 5, 1996. As she held him in her arms for the first time,

Pamela burst into tears and cooed, "Just look at his tiny fingers and toes. He's so precious. Oh, Tommy, I love him so much. Aren't we lucky?"

After the baby was born, Pamela rested for a day at home and then they took the baby to stay at a friend's home to avoid the photographers who had been camped out hoping to get a picture of Brandon. In six weeks she was expected back on the set of Baywatch, so she was going to grab every moment to bond with her baby boy.

Later, Pamela raved: "That was unbelievable, having a baby at home with a midwife. I never thought about going to the hospital and taking drugs for birth. I'm not going to break in half, even though it may feel like it. It was the most painful thing I ever experienced. I thought, 'I have a high tolerance for pain, I've got a couple tattoos.' That was the stupidest thing I ever thought: I can handle a tattoo, so I can handle childbirth."

Chapter 13

NOT EVEN THE DISMAL failure of Barb Wire could dampen the joy Pamela felt in becoming a mother at last. And what a failure Barb Wire was: The movie had been released on the first weekend of May and it was pretty much out of the theaters by the time Brandon arrived June 5, taking in only $4 million in the United States during its aborted run. Polygram, the studio who had backed the film to the tune of $18 million dollars, which included Pam's reported $750,000 salary, wrote the film off as a giant loss — and Pam's big-screen career with it.

"Her movie career is finished as far as we're concerned," said studio executive Stewart Till. "Barb Wire is a disaster for Polygram. We will not be working with Pamela again."

In the aftermath, Pamela dumped her lawyer and manager, installing Tommy as her new rep. And, after giving birth to Brandon, she did what she had to do: Pamela returned to Baywatch.

Like many first-time mothers, she didn't want to just leave her son at home with a nanny, so she set up a nursery filled with toys and diapers in her trailer on the set. "I've seen some of those Hollywood moms," Pam said. "They hardly see their children. I'm not going to be that kind of mother." She was also breast-feeding at the time, and that caused delays and at least one embarrassing moment. Once, when Pamela was filming a scene, the director suddenly called, "Cut!" Pamela, who always has her lines memorized and likes to rehearse a scene no matter how short before filming it, knew that she hadn't done anything to mess up the scene. She started looking around to see what was wrong and no one would look back. They were all looking away from her, a little embarrassed. That's when she looked down to see two wet patches on her bathing suit. "The milk was squirting from my nipples," Pam said about her overactive mamms. "Needless to say, I made a hasty departure to the trailer."

In spite of rumors that circulated about the baby causing short tempers on the set when he tested out his new lungs by howling, Pamela got the producers of Baywatch to pony up a cool $50,000 offer for Brandon to make his world television debut. The idea was simple: He would play an abandoned infant who is temporarily adopted by Pamela's character.

Despite this canny move, and a reported raise for Pamela to $60,000 per episode, there were still reports that she and Tommy were quickly headed to the brink of a financial abyss that would soon find them in bankruptcy court. Among their lavish expenditures: Six-figure sums spent on furniture and home improvements, $50,000 for landscaping,

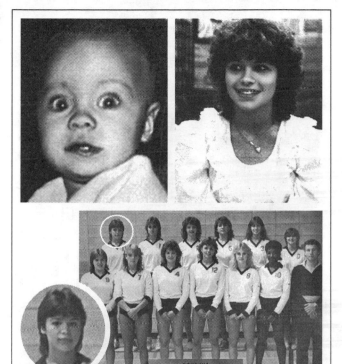

Bright-eyed baby Pamela Denise Anderson was born July 1, 1967; as a sophomore at Highland Senior Secondary School. Pamela (circled) on the 1983 all-star volleyball squad. In the 1985 yearbook, Pamela's senior class picture had a caption that said, prophetically, "Probable destiny: California beach bum."

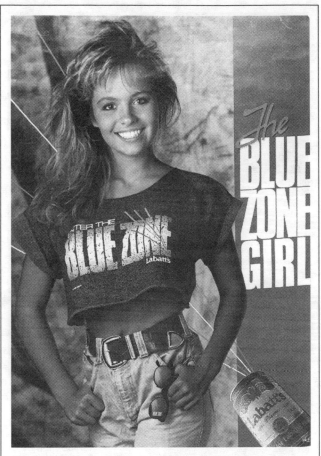

The
**BLUE
ZONE
GIRL**

Pamela was just another pretty face in the crowd at a British Columbia Lions football game when the image of her jumping up and down was flashed on a JumboTron in front of 50,000 fans. The crowd went nuts, she was brought down to the 50-yard line and introduced as "The Blue Zone Girl" because she was wearing a T-shirt for Labatt's Blue beer. The brewery made her an official spokesperson, launching a modeling career that has kept her in T-shirts and cutoffs – and less – for 15 years.

Pam turns comedian Tim Allen's head on the set of *Home Improvement* in which she played Lisa, The Tool Time Girl, for three seasons on the no. 1 comedy in the early '90s. At right is co-star Debbie Dunning.

"Somehow or other I always end up naked or in a bathing suit. And I don't even like to swim."

Pamela with the 1994 cast of Baywatch. Top: David Charvet, whom she dated, David Hasselhoff and Alexandra Paul. Bottom: Yasmine Bleeth, Jaason Simmons and Pamela Anderson.

Pamela Anderson and Happy Days star Scott Baio, her first Hollywood boyfriend, in 1990 (top left) and in 1993 (top right), the year they were engaged, but did not marry.

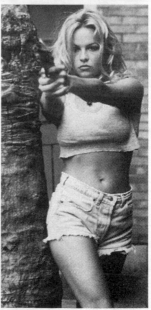

Pamela takes aim at a feature film career with Raw Justice. The 1994 action thriller was her second movie role and it missed the target, winding up on the video shelves as Good Cop, Bad Cop.

"I do as well as I can, but I'm not doing Masterpiece Theatre," Pam has said of her acting abilities. 1993's Snapdragon (top right) was Pamela's first film, in which she played Felicity, an amnesiac who kills her lovers. Pam on the Baywatch set (above) and in the famous red bathing suit.

She kissed, he told. Pam's seven-month fling with Bret Michaels of the "hair metal" band Poison turned toxic after an X-rated video of them surfaced in 1995. The same year, Pamela launched Barb Wire in a leather bustier at the Cannes Film Festival in France (right).

"It was instant, mindblowing animal attraction," Pamela said of Motley Crue drummer Tommy Lee. They were married in Cancun four days after their first date. Below and right, the ceremony took place on beach loungers and instead of wedding bands, they had each other's names tattooed on their ring fingers.

Fond of public displays of affection, Pam – who sometimes convinced her husband to put on her rubber dresses – gives Tommy a smooch for the cameras.

"Carrying a baby made me
feel like a real woman.
I wasn't a little girl anymore."

As the leather and bubble clad character in *Barb Wire*
(top and bottom), Pam was poised to bust out. The flick
flat-lined, earning only $4 million in five weeks in the
United States. "I don't care if I never make another movie
again," Pam said during the filming. To date, she hasn't.

Pam and Tommy could be raunchy (top) and romantic (above). They exchanged vows four times between 1995 and their 1998 divorce. The first time Pam wore a white bikini. The next, it was a silver space suit. Then she carried a head of lettuce for a bridal bouquet and finally she was married in a traditional wedding gown.

Tommy Lee first caught Pamela's attention on New Year's Eve 1994. According to the Motley Crue biography, The Dirt, Tommy licked the side of Playboy's favorite Playmate (with a record 10 covers) while under the influence of Ecstasy.

A devoted animal rights activist, Pamela fills out her
People for the Ethical Treatment of Animals T-shirt a
little less bountifully after the removal of her silicone
gel implants in early 1999.

If they gave awards to performers who made the most of awards show appearances, Pamela Anderson would undoubtedly earn a nomination. Right: Wearing his-and-hers bikinis, Pamela clowns with Damon Wayans at the 1999 World Music Awards in Monaco.

Pamela Anderson Lee, as she was known during her marriage, and her rock star husband, Tommy, bring up the rear on the red carpet of the 1996 MTV Video Music Awards.

Pamela dated pro surf champion Kelly Slater (above) before, during and after her three-year hitch with Tommy Lee. Supermodel Marcus Schenkenberg gave Pamela a 3-carat diamond engagement ring and she bought him a $75,000 Dodge Viper, but their romance lasted less than a year.

Of her golden globes, Pamela has said, "They have a career of their own and I'm just tagging along."

Party girl Pam makes a spectacle of herself (below) in movie star sunglasses with Elizabeth Hurley after the 2001 Academy Awards.

A glam Pam has her photo snapped at the Divas Live
concert where she met her current fiancé Kid Rock.
She has joked that her autobiography should be titled,
I Just Can't Think With All This Hair.

"My choices may seem crazy sometimes with men. I like to have fun. I don't need anybody for anything. A man in my life is just someone I want to be with instead of someone I need to be with."

Having fun (left) with Bob "Kid Rock" Ritchie (top and left).

After being diagnosed with life-threatening hepatitis C, the vegetarian performer went into semi-retirement to concentrate on her kids and health. "I'm a single mom with two young, beautiful children, and I just can't stand the thought of being in bed sick, missing out on spending time with them."

"I felt like I was Dolly Parton for the longest time," said Pamela, explaining why she had her implants removed in 1999. She had them put back in, obviously, after only a few months.

Pamela as the world knows her best, running slow motion on the beach. During its heyday, Baywatch was watched by nearly 2 billion people in over 140 countries.

Pamela with her sons, Dylan Jagger and Brandon Thomas: "I could lose everything, I could live in a box on the side of the freeway as along as I had my kids."

An animal lover, Pam received the first annual Linda McCartney Award from the People for the Ethical Treatment of Animals in 1999.

Pamela, who has ridden motorcycles in the film Barb Wire, may have trouble buttoning her jacket (left); but the most commercial cover girl of the 21st century has no problem taking a back seat when fiancé Kid Rock (below) is driving.

The tattoo below the birthmark on Pam's left arm is for Barb Wire. She claimed to have gotten hepatitis C from a tattoo needle she shared with Tommy Lee, whose tattooed name she had removed from her finger with a laser.

Pussycat Dolls Carmen Electra (who replaced Pamela on Baywatch), founder Robin Antin and Pamela Anderson heat up L.A.

"My public persona is a double-edged sword and I know I've played into it. The breasts, the blond hair, all the antics have made me a household name, but it's as much a curse as a blessing."

"My kids are hysterical," says Pam, feeding sons Brandon and Dylan and taking them on a bike ride. "They think every mom has a TV show and every dad is a rock star. They ask other kids, 'What band is your daddy in?' "

"It would be too difficult to try to create some sort of character for the world. I'm just me. When I tease my hair and put bright red lipstick on, I don't care what anyone else thinks," declares Pamela, who obviously gets no argument from Jay Leno.

Pamela and her intended Bob "Kid Rock" Ritchie, dressed to the nines for the opera in Vienna in February 2003. "I don't want to be one of those guarded, living in my shell kind of people," says Pamela, born under the sign of Cancer the crab. "I certainly haven't gone into this engagement blindly. Believe me, the last thing I ever imagined I'd do was marry another rock star."

not to mention the massive fish pond at their \$2 million Malibu mansion. There were her lingerie bills and his liquor tab and continuous legal expenses, the latest involving big bucks to defend Pamela against a breach of contract suit for allegedly pulling out of a commitment to make a movie called Hello, She Lied.

Meanwhile, Tommy continued to try to direct Pamela's career, even as he was spending them into the poorhouse. In an ill-fated move, he suggested to the newly reunited members of his old band Motley Crue that Pamela should make a guest vocal appearance on their comeback record. Pamela couldn't be bothered one way or the other and, perhaps to relieve the tension, she "kidnapped" her mate from the recording studio and flew him down to Cancun, the site of their first wedding. Once again, the ceremony was non-traditional. They were married for the third time by a bartender who moonlighted as a minister. Pam's bridal bouquet was a head of lettuce and the witnesses were two beer-guzzling patrons at the cocktail-shaking clergyman's bar.

When she returned to the states, Pamela announced that she had signed up for acting lessons with an acclaimed coach, Shawn Nelson, because she was tired of being known as a blond bimbo and didn't want her new son to grow up embarrassed by his mother. Her husband, unfortunately, had no such protective instincts. Back in the studio with Motley Crue, Tommy was on a tear again.

On Oct. 15, 1996, the drama-prone drummer was partying at the Viper Room, a club on Sunset Strip that became infamous as the scene of River Phoenix's death from a heroin overdose on Halloween night 1993. When he emerged from the club, photographer Henry Trappler was waiting, hoping to snap a picture. It was Tommy who snapped, however, throwing Trappler to the ground and breaking his hip and ribs. Trappler filed assault charges. Tommy got off easy with probation and anger management classes. But it was becoming evident to the world that the denials the Lees constantly issued about Tommy's violent temper were just that: denials.

It seemed like Pam had been sucked into the vortex of living in denial as well. She had given her all to her husband. She was the main breadwinner of the family, struggling to keep them financially afloat. Every time she tried reasoning with Tommy about his financial irresponsibility it led to a screaming match. Desperate to keep the cash flowing, she was persuaded by a guy who offered her husband $50,000 for Pam to make three test commercials for fat-reducing cream. She later regretted the commercials.

There were other disturbing whispers making their way around the Hollywood grapevine. Not only was Tommy a reckless spender who had only $100 in his checking account when he met his future wife, gossipmongers said he was also a notorious skirt-chaser and he hadn't slowed his pace one bit. When he wasn't out flirting with girls, Tommy was wreaking havoc on the domestic life Pam prized so much. Earlier in the year, he let Motley Crue guitarist Nikki Sixx crash at the Malibu house after he split up with his wife, turning the house into a messy bachelor pad. They would both stay out late and come home stinking of booze and other women's perfume.

Yet Tommy was openly indignant that he had to share the house with Pamela's parents, who were staying with her during her pregnancy and helping her decorate the new nursery for her first, long-awaited baby.

The situation hardly improved when Brandon arrived; Pam had to ask her parents to move out and only come to help with the baby during the day, but Tommy objected to that, too. Later Pamela would admit that her mom and dad had seen right through Tommy's tricks and were well aware of his transgressions. "My parents hated him and told me I was a fool to put up with his abusive behavior," she told a pal.

Things were no better at work. Whatever goodwill Pamela had with the cast and crew at Baywatch had long since evaporated in the wake of Tommy's fiery temper and pushy attempts to manage his wife's career. Pam's co-stars may have been sympathetic to her plight, but they knew there would be trouble when Tommy arrived on the set. Like Bret Michaels, Tommy couldn't make the separation between reel life and real life and he was convinced that every man Pamela did a scene with wanted to make love to her. In the latest series of episodes, Pam's character CJ had a new romantic interest on Baywatch, a buff blond guy named David Chokachi, and jealous Tommy flew into a rage every time the poor actor had to embrace or kiss Pamela.

And there was another new cutie on the Baywatch set who was trying to undermine Pam's position as queen of the sand. Her name was Donna D'Errico, and she was not only attempting to clone Pam's look, but she had also posed for Playboy in a layout that reminded many of Pamela's spreads. Donna even started dating Tommy's band mate, guitarist Nikki Sixx.

The worst humiliation was yet to come. Pamela was still reeling from the failure of Barb Wire when she started hearing that Hollywood insiders were raving about her performance in another movie — one that she and Tommy had starred in and directed themselves.

Chapter 14

IN THE HISTORY OF Hollywood, it may be the most famous stag film ever. Of course it was nothing new for actresses to be accused of having sex on camera, those rumors had plagued Joan Crawford and Marilyn Monroe throughout their careers. Some moviegoers were convinced that certain on-screen couples — such as Donald Sutherland and Julie Christie in the 1973 film Don't Look Now — hadn't been acting at all while making their love scenes. But in the age of the portable videocam, the Pam and Tommy video was a true landmark. It not only featured the biggest sex symbol in the known universe and her husband, but it was real and raw — completely uncensored and hardcore, with full frontal nudity, penetration and "money shots."

For anyone who still doubted that Pamela Anderson really allowed herself to be photographed having sex, that she carried a Polaroid of Bret Michael's penis, this was irrefutable proof. After all, a Polaroid, such as the one of Pam and Tommy enjoying each other's company that was published in the French edition of Penthouse and the U.S. sex rag Screw, could conceivably be doctored. But there was simply no denying that the videotape that had been bootlegged, passed around and screened in some of the finest homes in

Hollywood was of Pam and Tommy — in the flesh and going at it.

The existence of the videotape first came to public attention in early spring 1996. It was then that Pamela filed a $10 million lawsuit for humiliation, invasion of privacy and mental anguish against Bob Guccione, the publisher of Playboy's biggest rival, Penthouse. Guccione had received the tape from an unknown source while preparing a story about the Lees. Pamela was horrified to hear that Guccione planned to publish still photographs from the videotape, which, she testified in court documents, contained "explicit sexual and intimate relations, the private lovemaking of a husband and wife." Further, Pamela's claim was that Penthouse "has admitted that they intend to copy, publish, distribute and market the video for profit."

Pam claimed that she and her husband had locked the tape in a safe, which had been removed from the couple's home during renovations some time between October 1995 and January 1996. Pam even hired famed investigator Anthony Pellicano (who was involved in the Michael Jackson child molestation case, among others) to find out whodunit. Within a week of the announcement that Pellicano was investigating the theft, a $400-a-week member of the 40-man crew renovating the Lee's Malibu mansion stepped forward and admitted he'd lifted the hot property. He said he took it from the couple's VCR, not a safe, after he had been dismissed for peeking on Pam when she was taking a shower. The man claimed he then sold it to a photographer who subsequently sold it to Penthouse.

Pamela had earlier filed for an injunction barring Penthouse from publishing images from the video or selling the tape. She argued that the tape was stolen private property and that Penthouse had no right to profit from it, but a Los Angeles Superior Court ruled against her. It may have been a case of blind justice and the story might've had a different ending if Pamela had not been so well-known for posing nude. It certainly didn't help matters that when the earlier Polaroids had been published Pamela blew it off, saying "Whoa! I'm having sex with my husband. In the end, who cares? Just the fact that somebody would publish those photographs says more about them than it does about me." Apparently, the court believed that Pamela's open-door policy on talking about sex — and her sex life in particular — had created a legitimate interest in publications, even skin magazines, to report on it.

Penthouse published the pictures with an article describing the contents of the tape in the June 1996 issue. It instantly became one of the most sought-after artifacts in the history of celebrity. Bootleg copies were changing hands for vastly inflated prices. Radio raunchmeister Howard Stern was said to have paid well over $100 for his copy.

"This is the greatest tape I've ever seen in my life," Stern raved. "It's great not only because of the sex and stuff, and it's Pam and it's Tommy Lee, two famous people, and Tommy's penis is ridiculously out of control. But forget about that. What's cool about it is that you get to live their lives with them. And she's shaved all over and then Tommy is looking at her, and all of a sudden he goes, 'Baby, spread your legs for me.' And she does, man, and I'm right there with him."

Millions of Americans also wanted to be right there with him, but it would take over a year, and many protracted and expensive court proceedings, before the tape became available to the public. In Hollywood, however, it was the party favor of choice, shown at private screenings in peoples' homes and executives' offices. By June 1996, it had even been reported that Tommy's ex, Heather Locklear, stormed out of a party when the host stood in front of his VCR and announced he was about to slip the Triple-X treat in.

Not since Deep Throat — the 1970s adult film that introduced a generation to pornography and oral sex and made its star Linda Lovelace a household name

— had there been such a swell of interest in a movie with explicit sexual material. Since then, there have been sweeping changes in the American cultural landscape. With the arrival of VCRs, pornography became a boom industry, no longer relegated to seedy cinemas with dirty old men in raincoats. Now anyone could watch sexual films in the privacy and comfort of their own living room.

Pamela was devastated that the tape that she and her husband had made for their own amusement might possibly find its way onto the shelves of video stores throughout the world. Her career was already in a terrible state after Barb Wire and she knew that her future on Baywatch would be jeopardized if the tape was ever released. She knew full well what America would think. He would be the stud and she would be the slut. What really hurt Pamela was the rampant speculation that she and her husband had planned it all as an elaborate publicity stunt designed to boost both of their sagging careers.

Pamela lived silently with all of these fears — the sudden loss of her job on Baywatch, the tide of public opinion turning against her, the end of her career as an actress, possibly the end of her lucrative relationship with Playboy — hoping the tape would disappear.

By November, Pamela was at her wit's end, praying that the tape wouldn't go public and trying to steer her marriage and her career away from the rocks. She was getting no support from her sex-crazed, booze-soaked husband, either. In fact, Tommy seemed to be heading off the rails, getting higher than ever before and reaching new lows in partying and carrying on with women. One of them was a call girl in Heidi Fleiss' stable; another was a notorious porn star, whom Pamela caught in bed with her husband in the same house where she was raising Tommy's son.

Confronting him only made matters worse. He became verbally abusive, pushed and shoved Pamela and threatened her with serious physical violence. In desperation, Pamela even turned to David Hasselhoff and Heather Locklear for advice. Both of them were understanding, but also warned her to get out before she ended up like Nicole Simpson. On November 15, she bundled Brandon up and fled to her mother's house in Canada.

Four days later, Pamela Anderson filed for divorce.

Chapter 15

IN THE DAYS THAT followed, Pamela and Brandon took refuge at the $3 million Aspen Colorado ranch owned by producer Jon Peters. Pam was fearful that Tommy might come after her, but even so, still thought that he could be a good husband and loving father if only he could rid himself of the demons that drove him to drink and cheat. What she really wanted was for her family to be together. Thanksgiving was a couple of weeks away and the upcoming Christmas would be Brandon's first.

Tommy was shattered, too. He knew he had screwed up and was in danger of losing the two most important and loving people in his life. Pamela's actions had a sobering effect on him. Instead of drowning his sorrows, he began seeing a therapist and attending AA meetings and tried getting in touch with Pamela. Although she refused his calls, she issued an ultimatum through her lawyers. Pamela told him that she would only drop the divorce suit if he checked into rehab for drugs and alcohol.

One day, when she called to check in on him, she heard a heartfelt plea on the outgoing message on his answering machine. "Hi, it's Tommy. I'm not home right now, but I'll be back to you as soon as possible. If this is Pam, please come home. I love you and the baby with all my heart — and I'll do anything to get you to come back to me."

Pam reportedly listened to the message 10 times. They started talking again. He begged Pam to take him back. She begged him to get help. He agreed to go into rehab if she called off the divorce. He also agreed to go into couples' therapy.

There was another reason Pamela was in a forgiving mood. After leaving Tommy, Pamela felt ill. Then she noticed that the way she was feeling may not have been solely caused by heartbreak — it was oddly reminiscent of morning sickness. Pam took a pregnancy test. It turned out that she was carrying a child. Although a subsequent test revealed that it had been a false positive, Pamela believed it was a sign that she and Tommy should have another child.

The day before Thanksgiving, she met Tommy at her attorney's office. It was an emotional moment. Tommy got down on his knees and begged forgiveness, crying like a baby. "My head was telling me no," Pam would later recall. "But my heart melted."

Nevertheless, Pam wasn't taking any chances — she produced a two-page document for him to sign, a vow that he would stay off booze and keep away from other women. Pamela did not instantly drop the divorce charges, although for the time being, they held little importance. The marriage had lasted for 21 months, but only ground to a halt for a mere nine days. By Thanksgiving, the family was all having turkey dinner together again.

Later, Tommy told a radio station that he had been sober nearly two weeks. "I had to make a choice. I can have a beautiful family and a career and everything I ever wanted. Or I can drink myself into nowhere."

Pamela took this as a sign that he had come to his senses and finally realized how much she loved him and how much his family needed him. She thought she had to leave for the sake of Brandon, but in her heart she knew that there was a deep connection and whatever happened between them, he was still the father of her child. She hoped that Tommy would change, but, as the saying goes, "You really have to want to change."

Apparently, Tommy didn't want to change that much. Only a week after she moved back in, Tommy tried to kiss Pamela and she recoiled in horror. He smelled like another man: Jack Daniels. "You've had your second chance and you've blown it, Bozo," she screamed. Then she packed her clothes, grabbed Brandon and went to stay with her parents at the house she got them in West Hollywood.

Tommy may have slipped, but he was determined. He sobered up again and Pam continued to cheer him on, calling him "her knight in shining armor." Tommy even convinced her to remarry him, though the divorce proceedings had never really gone through. On Christmas Eve, he arranged for the two of them to exchange vows for the fourth time.

At 7:15 p.m., Dec. 24, 1996, Pamela heard an unusual sound coming from outside their Malibu home. It was a clanking metallic sound, nothing like a wind chime. When she opened the door, there was Tommy, dressed in a shiny metal suit of armor, on a trusty steed bedecked in Medieval armor and velvet blankets. Together they rode off into the sunset. Upon their return, Pamela slipped into a white wedding dress, the first time she had worn one, and after a ceremony in front of a minister, family members and friends, they were man and wife again. It was, she hoped, the beginning of a new life for them.

The week before, Pamela drew a deep breath and took a different kind of plunge. Contract negotiations for the next season of Baywatch had come to a deadlock. Pamela asked for a sizable increase in salary to $100,000 per episode, but the producers would not budge. So she announced that after five years, she would be leaving.

It was a risky move, considering her precarious finances and the fact that her career was not exactly in high gear, but Pam was determined to rebuild her marriage and raise the bar for herself professionally. Of course, she had some aces up her sleeve: Her going rate at Playboy was nearly 10 times the price she was asking for a single episode of Baywatch. And she had recently signed with a new talent agency who understood that, despite the fact that her big screen debut had tanked, Pamela Anderson had helped make Home Improvement the number-one show in America and Baywatch the number-one show in the world. Already Aaron Spelling, the creator of Charlie's Angels and Dynasty, had expressed interest in building a role for Pamela on a daytime soap opera called Sunset Beach.

In the days around Christmas, there was another element to Pam's new life that emerged. She had been attending prayer sessions at the Lake Shrine in Santa Monica, which is part of Self-Realization Fellowship, a spiritual group founded by the Indian guru Paramahansa Yogananda in 1920. There, in the soft glow of candles amidst the presence of people who practiced yoga and treated her with compassion, Pamela was beginning to find some peace. It was a place where she could go in a T-shirt and sweats, without having to put on her Pamela Anderson pout, and be accepted by people who understood that she was a human being with a broken heart and worried mind that needed comfort and healing. It was there that she could reconnect with the lessons her grandfather had taught her, there that she could nourish her spiritual side.

Unemployed and out of the public eye, except for a Pizza Hut commercial she did, donating her fee to various charities, Pam seemed content. Staying at home had certainly improved her rocky relationship with Tommy, who was becoming a much more patient father and experiencing his own creative rebirth, working on the new Motley Crue album. She had developed a battle plan for keeping her marriage and her man on track, hiring only men or unattractive middle-aged women to baby-sit Brandon, and keeping a copy of her divorce petition posted on the refrigerator. She was continuing her spiritual development, doing meditation and yoga.

She was not, however, taking the best care of her famous, fabulous body. Pamela was losing weight again. Eating minute amounts of high-protein foods and exercising vigorously — doing karate, kick-boxing, swimming, biking and Rollerblading for hours a day — she had dropped down to a mere 98 pounds. She had done this before, knowing that Tommy preferred her skinny, but soon the stories started circulating, questioning whether her diet and fitness routine and the stress of her roller-coaster relationship, had made Pamela anorexic and also asked if she would soon require hospital treatment.

Fans who tuned in to see her give a delightful performance guest-hosting Saturday Night Live couldn't make sense of those anorexia rumors. Getting her first good notices in quite some time, Pamela spoofed herself and Baywatch, looking as buxom and curvy as ever. If she was keeping a secret, it wasn't that she was starving herself.

Pamela Anderson was pregnant again.

Chapter 16

FINALLY, THINGS SEEMED TO be going the way Pamela always hoped they would. She and Tommy had gone on a second honeymoon to Bora Bora, where she got a tribal tattoo on her back and conceived a new baby. She was putting on weight and had the glow of impending motherhood. She was starting to feel like her old frisky self again, revealing to reporters that her thermostat was running hot again. "My sex drive is through the roof. That's great for Tommy. Even when my stomach gets huge, he'll find a way around it. There aren't any sharp corners left on any of the furniture," she added, suggesting that it had more to do with her biological needs than with safety-proofing the house for Brandon, who was now a toddler.

When she wasn't having sex with her newly well-behaved hubby, she was dreaming about it. "I'm not bisexual and have never wanted to be with a woman," she remarked, "but this pregnancy has been weird. For some reason I'm having sex dreams about Madonna."

Even her baby shower was a triple-X affair. To please Tommy, Pam hosted a very adult party where guests were asked to bring sex toys instead of stuffed animals and baby blankets. Male and female strippers who peeled down to diapers and then their birthday suits showed up to entertain the rowdy crowd, and as for the refreshments — there was no red meat or liquor.

Maybe it was karma. Maybe just bad timing. But in 1997, pregnant Pam found herself in court again, at the center of two lawsuits that played off her reputation as a sex symbol. The first case involved a cheesy movie that Pamela had turned down in 1994. It was called Hello, She Lied and it was to be produced for and broadcast on the Showtime cable network. The producers claimed that Pamela had made a verbal agreement to star in the erotic film and had backed out one week before the start date of the project because she wanted to make Barb Wire.

Pamela claimed that she had never signed a contract and walked off the project because she had not been given the script approval and the control over nude scenes that she had been promised. These scenes included a gratuitous nude lathering session in the shower and a simulated sex scene on a pool table.

In an attempt to humiliate her, the producer's lawyer told an L.A. courtroom, "Your honor, this is Pam Anderson. Pamela Anderson has never done a project outside television that did not have nudity."

Pam would not be so easily broken. She told the courtroom what happened to her while she was filming a sex scene with actor David Keith in the

1994 movie Raw Justice. "I was thrown around. I was scratched. I was bitten. I cried and went home. I called my mother. It was a horrible experience. I was told that I would never have to do anything that made me uncomfortable. But when I got to the set and I was scheduled to do a love scene between me and David Keith they said 'action' and he threw me around the room." She broke down and sobbed softly as she concluded, "It was a bad experience and it was only my second movie. I am now uncomfortable about doing those kinds of scenes unless it is a person I know."

The basis for the lawsuit was not whether Pamela had breached a contract. The producers went ahead and made the movie as Miami Hustle without the nude scenes Pam had objected to, putting Kathy Ireland in the role. When the film tanked, they decided to sue Pamela. "They tried to prove how much they lost by not using me," Pamela said. "They sued for $5 million and lost on every count."

Indeed, the judge found that she had never even agreed to do the movie, but the publicity was brutal. The hearings were broadcast on Court TV, which made Pam, who was still in her first months of pregnancy, extremely agitated. In the end, she was exhausted, and even though she did not have to pay or reach a settlement, she was significantly out-of-pocket for legal costs. "I spent $250,000 defending myself on something that was totally bogus," she complained bitterly.

While Pamela was struggling to keep her marriage together and her bank balance intact, Tommy was finally working again. Five years later, after Lee had arguably become the most famous member of the band, Motley Crue reunited with original singer Vince Neil, despite the fact that he had once claimed to have enjoyed Pamela Anderson's favors for a short period of time before she had met Tommy.

Motley Crue released their album Generation Swine and toured, disastrously. Once a stadium sensation, they had a hard time filling seats. The tour was constantly upstaged by bulletins from the Anderson-Lee front: the emergence of the stolen home video with its pornographic content and the rumors of violence.

It was a gruesome, ill-timed attempt at a comeback and caused nothing but trouble in the rocky relationship between Tommy and Pamela. Though he sang a song "Brandon," about their little boy while sitting at a white piano (as corny a gesture as ever there was for a heavy metal madman) the rest of the act was a horror show. While Motley Crue ran through their repertoire, the screens behind them were filled with images of dismemberment, death and Charlie Manson. Tommy frequently asked female members of the audience to flash him; they happily complied.

The shows were not only tasteless and raunchy, but well beyond rowdy. In October, after a concert in Greensboro, Tommy and band member Nikki Sixx were busted, accused of assaulting a security guard, who attempted to stop the crowd from rushing the stage at the band's urging. Though it indicated that Tommy had hardly scratched the surface of his anger problems, the incident — which would come back to haunt him later — was nothing compared to his next legal battle. That one, which involved both Tommy and Pam, was going to be even more costly, more stressful and more potentially damaging to Pamela's career and bank balance, which she could ill-afford since she had been on hiatus after leaving Baywatch.

The X-rated video that she and Tommy made on their post-wedding trip to Lake Mead, California, had found its way off the black market and into the hands of a young Internet mogul named Seth Warshavsky, who owned a Seattle company called Internet Entertainment Group. Warshavsky had already made a small fortune with sites that broadcast sexual material on the World Wide Web. Unlike the producers of Hello, She Lied, he was well-financed and had a crack team of lawyers and stood to make an obscene amount of money by broadcasting scenes from the illicit video on his Web sites.

The Lees went to the Superior Court of California Nov. 6, 1997, asking for an injunction against IEG, but failed to get what they asked for — a restraining order to prevent the company from providing the tape to its Internet subscribers. The attorneys for IEG argued that the Lees wanted to suppress "material that is of great public interest, which has been previously published and which the plaintiffs themselves have publicized extensively in the media during the past two years." They further added that it was "absolutely indisputable that the Lees have relentless, even aggressively, sought to publicize their sex lives, their sexual appetites, their sexual proclivities, and so forth." The judge ruled that Pamela and Tommy had undermined the claim of invasion of privacy by discussing the tape and its contents on Howard Stern's radio show. They had, according to the judgment, violated their own privacy.

All hell was about to break loose. On November 7, when Pam was in her eighth month of pregnancy, IEG made the tape available to members of the sites www.clublove.com and www.freelivesex.com and trumpeted the ruling as a triumph in the history of First Amendment rights. IEG played the tape for five hours, during which time they scored three times as many hits as usual on their site. Thousands of downloads were made and traded across the Internet before Pamela and Tommy agreed to let a third party arbitrator decide on the fate of the tape.

For three tense weeks, the case dragged on. Pamela, now in her ninth month, was beyond stressed. The complete tape was already being bootlegged by another Internet entrepreneur named Milton Ingley, who defied an injunction that was granted to the Lees to prevent him from selling copies of the tape. Ingley had been hawking the tapes since late September and claimed to have sold thousands of copies at $55 a pop. Rather than stop, he simply moved his base of operations to sex-friendly Amsterdam. "I don't think Interpol is going to be extraditing him for contempt of court," Lee's attorney Lucy Inman remarked.

Meanwhile, public interest in the tape was surging out of control. The show business bible Variety had already reviewed it, saying that Anderson and Lee "make passionate love what seems to be like ten times in a short span of time, one place more inventive than the next…A bootleg classic is born." Entertainment Weekly said, "For those who've seen the tape, there's amazement that the newlyweds could film each other while flagrante delicto (in a moving car and a boat no less) and awe at their unselfconscious love. Pamela and Tommy seem so proud of their bodies, rumors persist that they made the tape with plans to cash in on it themselves." However, the entertainment magazine concludes, "Anyone who sees the tape would surely be startled at the idea it was staged. There's a naturalness in Pamela's demeanor — whether during sex or opening presents — that can't be found in her 'legit' work."

After everything she had been through, all the domestic dramas and professional setbacks, this was the nightmare from which she could not wake up. Pamela was completely drained. When she learned that IEG's attorneys were planning to take depositions from friends and associates, including David Hasselhoff and Tommy's ex-wife, Heather Locklear, the exhausted mom-to-be agreed to drop the arbitration proceedings and enter into a settlement with IEG.

Just let it be over, she thought.

In fact, it was only beginning.

Chapter 17

THE SETTLEMENT WITH IEG was signed, sealed and delivered by the first week of December. Pam was wiped out and retreated to her home in Malibu to wait for a more important delivery — her second son, Dylan Jagger Lee, named for rockers Bob Dylan and Mick Jagger, arrived at 11:20 a.m. Dec. 29, 1997, weighing in at a healthy 6 pounds, 14 ounces. As before, Pamela delivered at home with the help of a midwife and her husband, Tommy, who was her coach.

Nothing could spoil the elation Pamela felt in those first few weeks that she became a new mom all over again. Not the speculation that she and Tommy's settlement with IEG would make them millionaires, nor the news that there was another nasty videotape about to surface, one that she had made with her former boyfriend Bret Michaels. Not even the fact that IEG had written the settlement in such a way that they felt it would be reasonable to start selling the tape via mail order.

That's exactly what IEG did. Suddenly, anyone with $34.95 could purchase the 39-minute tape or rent it from a video store that had bought a copy. Hundreds of thousands did — in over a year it would generate $10 million in sales — just to see what all the fuss was about.

Pam & Tommy Lee: Hardcore & Uncensored

begins innocently enough, with scenes of the couple in Pam's dressing room on the set of Barb Wire. Pam is interrogating a hairdresser, whose face and voice are obscured to protect her identity, asking her about the size of a man's "wenis." There is a shot of Pamela in bed, on her 29th birthday, asking Tommy not to film her because "I have an ovarian cyst." There is the moment when he leads her blindfolded down to the yacht he chartered for her birthday and a scene in which Pamela opens her presents and thrusts them toward the camera.

Before they head off on another boating trip to Lake Mead, Pamela mans the camera, filming her dogs and her husband. She is in a randy mood.

"When are you going to get me preggos?" she asks. "Come on, whip it out."

He doesn't. But as they drive the Chevy Suburban, he reaches into his lap and exposes his manhood. It soon becomes erect. Pamela fellates him. "I get this for the rest of my life, kids," she says, gripping his erection and waving it toward the camera she is operating. "Mom is a lucky camper."

Tommy is overwhelmed. "F**k," he exclaims. "I'm so f***ing horny."

Pamela agrees. "We have to pull over. I can't stand it any longer. Baby, I want you."

Later, we join them on a rented houseboat. It is a

mess. They are drinking champagne and cocktails, calling each other "Lover," swearing undying love. Tommy is standing nude on the deck, you can hear Pamela compliment him on the size of his equipment, which he then tucks between his legs. "Yuck," she screams. "I hate that."

"Spread your legs for me," he requests, having taken over camera duties. She complies. Though the camera jiggles, it is clear that he is penetrating her.

When they have finished Pamela says, "I'm getting f***ing nailed three or four times a day. I've got to be preggos. I have to be preggos because you are so f***ing far inside me that it is beyond hurting."

"That'll be good when we show our parents the tape," Tommy observes wryly.

"Your parents might be proud that they have a very healthy well-endowed son," she replies.

On another afternoon, Tommy goes fishing. Pamela shrieks, "Oh, I feel so bad, I feel so bad," as the fish her husband has caught flops around on the deck of the boat. Tommy examines it, thinking it's too small to keep. "He's dead already, baby," Pamela says helpfully,

It is Day Three at Lake Mead, so a title card tells us. There is more sex, this time fellatio and vigorous intercourse with extreme oaths of love exchanged between the newly married lovers. Tommy ejaculates toward the camera. The scene is repeated in slow-motion as it would in a porno film. His face is twisted in ecstasy as corny piano music plays.

Wherever Tommy goes, whatever he does, Pamela follows him with the camera, shouting, "I love you," if he so much as leaves the room.

They scream each other's names and listen to their voices echoing off the rocky cliffs surrounding the lake. They play with an orange filter, sliding it on and off the lens, making goofy comments like two youngsters who are shooting their first video.

Tommy jumps off the boat, naked except for sneakers, and pulls it to a sandy shore.

"This is Nymphomaniac Island," Pam narrates. "Beware!"

"We're so camping, it's ridiculous," says Tommy.

They build a fire and take turns playing guitar.

Pamela grows pensive. She is sure they're being watched. "If anybody finds this tape, we're dead," she says eerily. "It's because a mountain lion was just over there somewhere." She laughs. "But Tommy will probably hit him or something if he comes over here so we can be sued by the f***ing wildlife organization."

At almost a dollar a minute, Pam & Tommy Lee: Hardcore & Uncensored, was pretty poor value. It was amateurish and idiotic, pretty much proving Pam's point that it was made for the couple's own collection, that it was no different than the kind of tapes almost "everybody's done at least once in their life." Held to the standard of even the cheapest adult videos, it offered very little — less than five minutes of actual sex and some exceedingly inane filler. Had anyone else made the tape it would not have been worth anything, but this was an internationally famous TV star and her equally renowned musician husband. And in the history of pop culture, there had never been such a widely distributed, widely viewed document of a celebrity's sexual adventures. Pamela Anderson became the first sex symbol to do more than just symbolize sex — she performed it with an abandon that proved she had earned her position as the most fantasized-about woman in the world.

In the future, historians may point to the last years of the 20th century as the time when American culture lost its last shred of sexual innocence. Executives and Joe Lunchboxes alike can eat lunch and flirt with buxom ladies at restaurants called Hooters, college coeds can put themselves through school by doing lap dances in strip clubs, teenage pop stars can get implants and piercings all over their bodies. Even the president of the United States did naughty things with cigars to interns who wore thongs.

Pamela Anderson added something else to the equation. She was now, literally, sex incarnate.

Porn stars like the notorious Traci Lords had already crossed over into mainstream movies. Through no intention of her own, Pamela Anderson reversed that trajectory and most people who viewed the tape came to a sudden realization that however she may have presented herself in the past, no actress could have been better suited to make such a startling transition.

There would be hell to pay for this. And it would be Tommy Lee who handed Pamela Anderson the bill.

Chapter 18

HE SHOULD'VE BEEN THERE for her. It was her reputation and her career that was going to be forever tarnished by that stupid tape. When Pamela renewed her vows with Tommy on Christmas Eve 1997, he promised to love and honor, to cherish and protect her. Yet in the days and weeks of the videotape ordeal, Tommy was not consumed with what he had done or what the tape could be doing to them, but what Pamela had done years earlier, also on videotape, with Bret Michaels.

"Tommy called me a whore and a slut and every rotten name he could think of," Pamela confided to a friend. "He was a raving maniac. I had to run and lock myself in the bedroom while he screamed and kicked the door. Sometimes it took two hours for him to calm down. Other nights I'd be sound asleep, he'd get up, turn on the tape and watch Bret and me making love together. Then he'd get drunk and come screaming into the bedroom, bottle in hand, waking up the kids and calling me foul names. Tommy claimed I should have warned him the tape existed before we were married."

If 1997 had been a pretty good year for Pamela and Tommy (at least they had gotten back together and he was trying to stay sober), 1998 was shaping up to be the worst ever. Tommy had been sober for nearly a year, but around Thanksgiving 1997, he slipped back into having a glass of wine every so often.

While many women suffer from postpartum depression, commonly known as the "baby blues," a new arrival in the family is often just as stressful and emotionally unbalancing for the husband. Tommy's behavior after Brandon's birth was initially giddy. It had been a long labor and he had been there every minute, coaching Pam by telling her how brave she was. In the days afterward, the adoring father cradled his son in his arms and posed for family pictures, looking like a goofball with a giant pacifier in his mouth. He had made elaborate plans for his son, buying him drums, talking about getting special leather diapers and having black clothes specially made, thinking about all the things he could teach him about rock 'n' roll, motorcycles and guns.

But as the novelty wore off and the monotony began, all of those days seemed so far off they might as well have been another lifetime. Feedings, changing diapers, calming Brandon down when he cried and rarely getting enough sleep took a toll on the family and there was another thing: Now Tommy had to share Pamela with another guy who was even more needy.

Five months after Brandon was born, Tommy's behavior became so intolerable that Pamela filed for divorce again. There was no reason to suspect that he wouldn't go through the same erratic cycle now that Dylan had arrived. With a new baby, Tommy felt the need to escape and, when that happened, the drinking accelerated. That other videotape, the one she made without him, was eating Tommy alive and now he had two kids clamoring for his wife's attention.

As jealous as he was over the Bret Michaels tape, he was also a man with a legendary sex drive. He wanted some alone time with his wife and knew that a little romance would go a long way.

Tommy Lee was a big Rolling Stones fan; after all, he named his second son Dylan Jagger Lee. So it was no surprise that he scored tickets to see the Stones play in Las Vegas in February 1998 and decided to take Pamela to the concert. It was to be the first time they'd been away alone since Dylan was born; it was also the month of their anniversary and Valentine's Day. At the concert, Tommy guzzled Cristal straight from the bottle. Afterward, they were photographed leaving the concert with Tommy still clutching the bottle and Pamela wearing a miniskirt and a cropped T-shirt that said "Girls Rule." Apparently Tommy agreed. At a party at the Hard Rock Hotel, a girl approached his table. Pamela had excused herself to visit the ladies' room and when she returned, she saw the woman peeling off her clothes and Tommy cheering her on. Pam slapped him across the face. He shoved her back, knocking her into some chairs, then chased her into the ladies' room, where they screamed at each other for 10 minutes before cooling down.

When they reached the tenth floor, where they had a $500-a-night suite, the fight started again. Tommy pushed Pam into a wall, put her in a headlock and ripped her shirt off in the hallway, exposing her breasts. The fight continued in the suite. Tommy smashed a lamp and chased Pam, who had barricaded herself in the bathroom. Undeterred, Tommy kicked a hole in the door and then broke it open. He put Pamela in a headlock again and then threw her to the ground in the bathroom. Pamela screamed and begged him to stop hurting her. Finally, as she collapsed in tears, he staggered out of the bathroom and passed out on the bed.

After a couple of hours, Pamela collected herself, ran to her assistant's room down the hall and exclaimed, "Get me out of here!" At 5 a.m. she left the Hard Rock Hotel and took the private plane they'd chartered back to Los Angeles, leaving Tommy stranded, sleeping it off in their trashed suite. When she got home she grabbed her kids and her parents, who had been watching them, threw some clothes in a plastic bag and checked into a hotel.

Pamela had very much been looking forward to

the Las Vegas trip. "It was a romantic little getaway," Pamela explained. "I walked into the room and he had rose petals all over the floor, and bottles of champagne. And I went 'OK, there's a lot of champagne around here.' "

Pamela has often said that she doesn't like the out-of-control feeling that alcohol produces in her, but she drank champagne that night. What she remembered was that she was weaning Dylan from breast-feeding and feeling sore, and her crying got Tommy angry. That was the first time he got physically violent toward her. Pamela would later say that it was as if he had "lost his mind. He went completely blank. His eyes were glass. I didn't know who he was when he was doing that."

Tommy returned the next day, tail between his legs. Pam suggested that they go to therapy, though it was clear he was the one who needed the most help. In the back of her mind, she was already thinking that they would split up, but she agreed to couples therapy for the sake of her marriage and her kids. According to Pam, the therapist told Tommy that one way to determine if he was an alcoholic was to limit his intake to two drinks a night.

That would not end up a particularly good idea.

Chapter 19

VALENTINE'S DAY WAS RUINED. Pamela had taken Tommy back, but she was miserable and riddled with anxiety, wondering when the next explosion would occur. She hadn't quite lost all hope of keeping her family together — after all, Tommy was going to get help and she knew that deep down inside he still loved her — and she also prayed that she wasn't going to have to raise her family alone. There were voices in her head. "Get out now," one whispered — while another asked, "What about the children?"

Pamela had always said she was crazy about Tommy, and maybe that's what it was — a kind of romantic insanity. Perhaps she even felt that somehow she was to blame for Tommy's behavior. As much as she was physically shaken, the toll that the fight in Las Vegas had taken on her was even more intensely psychological. For someone who had changed her life so radically, who had actually left a small town and conquered Hollywood just by making the most out of the opportunities that came her way, by having the confidence to live out her fantasies, Pamela Anderson was suddenly overcome with doubt.

There would be no more doubt after the evening of Feb. 24, 1998. That was the night that Pamela would get absolute proof that she was in real trouble.

Pamela and Tommy were at home with the kids. He had opened a bottle of wine and had his two glasses, which only put him in a foul mood. He was still boiling over the Bret Michaels tape and the fact that Pam had ditched him in Vegas.

According to Tommy's account in The Dirt, he was looking for a particular pan to stir-fry vegetables. When he couldn't find it, he started throwing pots and pans back in the drawer.

"And then Pamela said the words that you should never say to anyone...'Calm down. You're scaring me.'

"That was it. We were off and running. She screamed at me, I screamed back at her and pretty soon the kids started screaming."

Tommy wrote that she picked up the phone to call her mother. He hung up the phone. Twice. "She threw the phone against the handset, clenched her fist and swung at me blindly, connecting half the fist with my lower jaw and the other half with the tender part of my neck. I had never been hit by a woman before and as soon as I felt the contact, I saw red."

According to Pamela, however, she had tried her best to be the understanding wife. "I thought he needed some attention from me," she recalled. "That's a real thing with men and new babies. It's almost like he had postpartum." And he wasn't helping out with the kids and that meant she had to do it, which meant she couldn't be with him.

So Pamela suggested calling her parents and having them come by and help with the kids. This infuriated Tommy, who spat out, "They're here all the time. You don't give me any attention and you don't love me anymore."

Pamela tried to calm him. "That's not true," she countered. "I do love you. You need to calm down."

Pamela finally thought, "Enough, already!" She remembered what her therapist told her — that Tommy was not her child. He was her husband and he was supposed to be a helpful and equal partner in marriage and parenting. The therapist had told Pamela that when Tommy got needy and childish, she should turn on her heel and just walk away.

That proved to be a bad move. When Pamela turned away, Tommy exploded. He was throwing pots and pans around in the kitchen and rocking back and forth on the floor like a spoiled brat having a temper tantrum.

He started raging and chased her into the children's room. The kids started crying and as she tried to hold them in her arms, Tommy kicked her twice. She fell against the wall and 2-month-old Dylan bumped his head. "He could have done anything at that point," Pamela realized. "What really frightened me was that he had no regard for his children. The babies were crying and hyperventilating; and I was shaking and screaming and holding both the babies when he kicked me in the back. I thought, 'There's nothing I can do if he's not even listening to his children.' "

It was 7:45 p.m. when Pamela dialed 911.

By the time the police arrived, Tommy's storm had blown over — he had gone from rage to pitifully begging. He pleaded with Pamela, trying to convince her not to press charges. The officers discovered the phones had been ripped off the wall, expensive pieces of crystal were smashed and scattered on the floor, and the kids were crying inconsolably.

The report that the police filed referred to Pamela as V (victim) Lee and Tommy as S (suspect) Lee, and read like this:

V/Lee was holding her son (Dylan, 7 weeks) in her left arm. V/Lee punched S/Lee in the upper right chest area with her right fist in an effort to get away from S/Lee. V/Lee broke free from S/Lee's grasp and fled into the children's room. S/Lee followed and kicked V/Lee in the left buttocks...This caused V/Lee to lose her balance and fall into a chalkboard hanging on the wall. Dylan's head struck the chalkboard eraser shelf. S/Lee then grabbed his other son (Brandon, 20 months) and started to leave the location. V/Lee feared for

Brandon's safety due to the fact that S/Lee had been drinking.

V/Lee followed S/Lee in an attempt to retrieve Brandon. S/Lee grabbed V/Lee's right index finger with his right hand and twisted. This partially ripped V/Lee's fingernail from the fingernail bed, causing it to bleed…Fearing for her boys' and her own safety, V/Lee dialed 911.

Pamela told police that Tommy had also grabbed her jaw and squeezed it powerfully. They noted her injuries and investigated the scene, finding a semi-automatic weapon near the couple's bed, which was a violation of Tommy's earlier probation for the assault on the photographer outside the Viper Room club on Sunset Strip in October 1996. Now Tommy was looking at some serious trouble: violation of his probation and unlawful possession of a firearm — convictions that could put him away for up to seven years.

Pamela stood firm and said she was going to file charges as Tommy was handcuffed and taken to jail. According to a guard there, "He was a sniveling wimp" and cried like a baby. He would be there for three days until he was released on $500,000 bail on the condition that he immediately be enrolled in an anger management program and that he would under no circumstances try to contact his wife, kids or in-laws. He moved in with Motley Crue's Nikki Sixx.

In the meantime, Pamela moved quickly and decisively, getting an emergency protection order to keep Tommy away from her and the kids. She changed the locks on the house in Malibu, hired a security team and took shelter with her producer friend Jon Peters, shuttling back and forth between two of his homes that had high-tech security systems. This time she had no intention of turning back on her divorce proceedings.

In the days that followed, Pamela's bruises were beginning to heal, but she often felt dizzy and had chronic headaches. It wasn't until she went to the dentist that Pamela discovered that these symptoms had nothing to do with the anxiety she felt, but that she was suffering from TMJ, also known as temporomandibular joint disorder. The agonizing condition had been caused when Tommy knocked her jaw out of alignment during their brawl in Las Vegas. Pam revealed to a friend, "I knew he'd really hurt me in Las Vegas. It wasn't the first time he'd decked me, but this time I heard a kind of click and felt a searing pain. That was definitely the start of the problem. I'm still finding out about the physical damage that he's caused me. My jaw ached and was badly swollen after he punched my face. Every time I took a bite to eat, it hurt." This was the same condition that afflicted Burt Reynolds back in 1984, causing him to lose so much weight that people speculated he was wasting away from AIDS.

While the physical pain was intense, the even greater psychological injury Pamela was suffering from was much harder to pin down. At its worst, she felt completely unsafe, terrified that Tommy "could O.J. me," as she put it. Despite around the clock protection, she knew that with Tommy out on bail anything might happen and she took to wearing disguises if she had to go out in public. She was afraid to let even her closest friends know where she was staying, for fear that Tommy would threaten them.

Pamela was also concerned about the impact that witnessing such violence might have upon Brandon, who was going to be two in a few months. If there was one bright spot in her life, it was that her kids seemed to be doing OK. Although she was still feeling betrayed, it helped to have these little darlings to shower with love and care for.

There was also another emotion roiling deep inside her — Pamela Anderson was angry. "I'm not going to be a victim anymore," she vowed to her friends. She went public with her story, unashamed to tell the world what had happened to her, in the hope that it might help other victims of domestic abuse and give her a way to release some of her own fury. It was not something she had planned to do and probably not something she was advised to do, since people in Hollywood can be masters of sweeping things under the carpet. Yet somehow, Pamela found the strength.

As a result, something unexpected happened. As she told her side of the story, a horrifying pattern of abuse emerged and despite the appearance of the X-rated videotape, Pamela started to win sympathy and respect. People who had written her off as a dumb bimbo were now beginning to see her as an articulate hero. Some even speculated that she made the videotape to satisfy a husband who could never really be happy with anything his wife did for him.

After her ordeal, Pamela tapped into an inner strength to keep her head up, to pull herself and her children through the pain and the fear and to carry on. And she was rewarded by this newfound public support.

She would need it. On March 4, less than two weeks after her beating, Pamela had to give a deposition to lawyers about the Bret Michaels videotape. IEG, the company that had released Pam & Tommy: Hardcore & Uncensored, were also bringing her to court claiming that she had gone on several talk shows and done interviews saying that IEG had no right to sell the tape. Suits and countersuits over whether IEG did have that right, whether Pamela was not in compliance with the terms of the settlement that had been reached, and who, in fact, was defaming whom, were being discussed and prepared. It was an expensive and ugly legal nightmare.

It was not the only one, either. Tommy was due in court April 7, 1998, to answer to numerous charges including battery, unlawful possession of a firearm and child endangerment. Judge Mira, who had sent Robert Downey Jr. to jail for violation of his probation said:

Lee did willfully and unlawfully under circumstances likely to produce great bodily harm and death, injure, cause and permit a child, Dylan Lee to suffer and be inflicted with unjustifiable physical pain and mental suffering having the care and custody of said child injured and did willfully cause and permit said child to be placed in such a situation that his person and health were endangered.

On April 7, Tommy pleaded no contest to a felony charge of spousal battery. It would be over a month before he was sentenced and, during that time it was announced that Pamela, who had toned down her appearance under the guidance of fashion designer Marc Bouwer, would be starring in a syndicated television series due to premiere in the fall.

On May 20, 1998, Tommy Lee stood in front of Judge Mira again. He was ashen-faced and wearing a pinstriped suit. Tommy was sentenced to six months in jail for battery. It was a suspended three-year prison sentence conditional upon him spending 180 days in jail and paying a total of $6,200 to a battered women's shelter, a victim restitution program and a domestic violence fund. He was placed in counseling and rehabilitation programs and was ordered to perform 200 hours of community service. He was not allowed to own guns and drinking alcohol or using drugs would be considered violations of the terms of his probation. Having violated an earlier probation, he was also warned that any violation of his probation after serving the six-month sentence would result in a three-year term in state prison.

"What I see here is a very clear — very disturbing in my judgment — pattern of conduct in which otherwise resolvable matters are handled by violence," said Judge Mira, noting that Tommy had been repeatedly put on probation for violent incidents dating all the way back to 1983. "You do it whether it's a family member or a third party. That's intolerable in any kind of civilized society."

Tommy turned to his parents, sister and friends and simply said, "See you later, guys." He was handcuffed and taken to Men's Central jail, where he was locked up in his own 8-by-8 foot cell. There was no special treatment because of his celebrity; but Tommy was kept away from the general population to protect him from other prisoners who might try to even the score on Pamela's behalf.

After the conviction, Pamela said, "I'm very happy that he took responsibility for this. I think it's the first step toward healing."

It was a generous thing to say, and Pamela meant it. In spite of everything he had done, she still had feelings for Tommy and she still had hope that they could work things out.

Chapter 20

PAMELA HAD A LOT to work out for herself. For a start, she had signed a contract to star in as well as executive produce the television show V.I.P. J.P. Lawton got hooked up with Pamela Anderson in the most mundane way known to Hollywood players — they were both represented by the same talent agency, William Morris. Lawton had the perfect pedigree to work with Anderson on her new television project: As a screenwriter, he wrote Pretty Woman for Julia Roberts and Under Siege for Steven Seagal, so he obviously had an appreciation for hot women and action heroes. He even enjoyed Pamela's performance in Barb Wire, though he thought it was a pretty thankless role.

Then he saw her on the Tonight Show with Jay Leno. It was the first time he had thought about her as a human being instead of a blow-up doll. She had broken up with Tommy for the first time and had to answer a lot of questions, and Lawton was struck by her combination of honesty and dignity. He had also heard her on the Howard Stern show and was pleasantly surprised at how well she could hold her own with the filthy-minded shock-jock. It all boiled down to this: "Wow, this woman is no dummy."

Lawton thought that if someone could capture the funny, natural quality that Pamela brought to talk shows and write a character that played to those strengths, the results could be magic. So, in the early spring of 1997, they met. Lawton recalled that during that time Pam was being fussy about what her next project was going to be and had rejected everything her agency brought to her. His original intention was to take her Barb Wire character and add a sense of humor. She would be a bodyguard to the stars and an expert on every gun and every car.

Pam, however, didn't want to ride down that road again and suggested that the character be a fish out of water, a smalltown girl who accidentally becomes the head of a bodyguard agency, even though she doesn't know what she is doing. If it reminded the public of her days as the girl from the Canadian backwater who arrived in Hollywood and became a star, the resemblance was intentional. Pam wanted a departure from Baywatch, which had made her an international star, and Barb Wire, which was a global disaster. "Instead of being a straight action-adventure show or running down the beach in bathing suits thinking we're a really hot show, we poke fun at ourselves," she reasoned. "I think women have deadlier weapons than guns," said the woman looking like she was carrying loaded .38s. "Like humor."

They came up with an idea for a pilot. Pamela would play Vallery Irons, who comes from a small town and gets thrown into a life of prestige and glamour. She is working at a hot dog stand one day and a guy asks her out. He is Brad Cliff, movie star. She expects this guy to be really courageous and macho, but when a guy pulls a gun on him at a premiere, he throws her in front of him as a shield and cowers behind her. Vallery ends up accidentally kicking the gun out of the assailant's hands, the paparazzi go nuts and, to save face, Brad Cliff introduces her as his personal bodyguard. Cliff hires Vallery as the head of his security agency, promising her she'll never have to actually leave the office. Of course, she somehow always ends up in the middle of something awful.

"I really relate to the character," Pamela said. "It's kind of what goes on in my real life. Dodging bullets. I'm always in the middle of trouble."

They had no trouble selling it. Pam went to a convention and met with all the station owners and shook hands and took pictures. She went right up to them and said, "Put on my show." By the time she was finished, 98 percent of them had agreed and she had a commitment to shoot 44 hour-long episodes.

Anyone who had ever doubted Pamela's intelligence and ability to market herself was very impressed. Pam had picked up quite a lot of knowledge seeing David Hasselhoff transform Baywatch from a failed network series to the most successful television show ever. V.I.P. was budgeted at $1.3

million per episode. "I have really had to become the Big Bad Businesswoman," she said, clearly relishing the role. "This show is perfect for me. I'm producing it, so I get to decide just how ditzy Vallery acts, I get to decide when to put on a bathing suit and I get to decide if I save everyone."

No matter how much he had put her through in the past, the one person Pamela seemed intent upon trying to save was Tommy. She still had mixed feelings, torn between her love for him and her need to take care of her self and her children. "Picking up that phone [and dialing 911] was the hardest thing I ever did in my life," she said. "But I had to protect the kids. I've never been so afraid."

And yet, she did it. She turned him in. "He's going to be doing some jail time," she said sadly. "I don't know how jail will help; it should be more rehabilitative instead of punitive but maybe that's what he needs. He was 16 when he became a massive rock star and he's just used to having whatever he wants whenever he wants it. And he's just learning now that things have consequences."

It had consequences for her, too. Filing for divorce for the second time smashed Pamela's illusions about marriage. "I think every girl grows up with the fantasy of marriage and they always think Prince Charming is gonna come along and it's all gonna be wonderful for the rest of your life. I know that's not necessarily the case," she said.

And she was lonely. "I catch myself some days, really missing Tommy," she admitted. "And wanting to go to his rescue like I always have. But then I tell myself, 'That obviously doesn't work — it's his trip and there's nothing you can do.'"

Tommy went to jail shortly before production began on V.I.P. Pamela told her two young sons nothing more than that he was somewhere very important and that he loved them and would see them soon. She and Tommy were in contact, speaking every two weeks. Sometimes they had a three-way, talking with their therapist refereeing on the phone. "He wants very badly to have his family together and to be a father to his kids," she revealed. "I don't know about that, but I know he's going in the right direction."

In July 1998, V.I.P. was in full production mode. Pamela would take her two sons, Brandon and Dylan, to the set with her, where she had set up a nursery and play area in her office and her location trailer. As a producer and the star of the show, she kept long hours and didn't want her boys to be left in the care of nannies. After Brandon was born, her parents moved to California, setting up house nearby in Malibu. When Tommy left and the show began, they moved in with her to help out.

She was, for all intents and purposes, a single mom and a very busy one, and the men in her life were her two boys, co-workers and friends. Nothing romantic. In many ways, despite all her fears, her heart still belonged to Tommy.

V.I.P. was the name of Pam's bodyguard agency on TV: Vallery Irons Protection. It was a good name because it had a double meaning — most of the clients that her character looked after were V.I.P.s (Very Important People). But the title would come to have other meanings. In this very intense period, Anderson had herself become a V.I.P. A very introspective Pam. Alone, without a man, she had plenty of time to consider other V.I.P.s: very intimate problems like vastly invalidated promises and violence-induced paranoia.

Sure, she was busy raising two young sons and working on a television show that was supposed to point her floundering career back toward the mainstream, as well as working for the financial security of her family. But there was also a lot of time to think. Pamela was in therapy, seeing spiritual advisers and trying to gain some perspective on her life.

Pamela was no stranger to the couch. She was seeing a female psychologist at the time who became a role model to her. The woman told Pamela that she had so many people pulling her in so many different directions because she had herself been the caretaker of so many people. It wasn't just her fellow employees on V.I.P. who were counting on her for their jobs and her children but also Tommy, who was a child himself, and her parents and brother, too. So the psychologist gave Pamela a mantra. When people are trying to take advantage of her, she was supposed to say to herself: "Shut the f**k up."

"I learned through therapy you have choices in every second of life," Pamela observed. "And they can instantly change your life. Look what happened in my relationship. It doesn't take long to change the rest of your life. His life has been changed forever, my life has been changed forever, the children's lives have been changed forever, all because of a choice that he made in an instant."

Pamela had come to realize that their relationship was "a real tragic kind of sad love story gone bad. We had so much passion and love. It's just that the few things that were bad were really bad. I can't be in an unpredictable, unsafe situation.

"I'll always love him," she confessed. "I just don't have to live with him."

Pamela expressed compassion and support for her abusive spouse. "I married him and had children with him," she said. "He's a beautiful man, but there's a few bad things and those are too big to ignore." Having children made all the difference. "You just can't have a child growing up in a situation seeing that it's OK to treat women that way because they're going to grow up that way. I grew up that way, with my father being abusive to my mom. They grew through it, stuck it out, but although my Dad has mellowed out, they're still not a really happy couple. My mom has grown up with this bitterness — she has a lot of resentment from years ago. She's part of the reason I've been strong about Tommy."

Growing up, Pamela thought, "I am never gonna be with someone who hits me. My mom had me when she was 18 and my dad was 20. I think it was, like, a shotgun wedding. The problems with drinking and violence they had when I was growing up — I really felt like they were partly my responsibility because I felt like I was the reason they had to get married. I grew up seeing a certain style of relationship. I thought everyone had that in their family and I didn't take it as anything different. Maybe that's what I thought love was.

"My first love relationship in high school was really violent. You know when you're growing up and you gravitate toward how you grew up, just unconsciously? I've had plenty of nice men ask me to marry them, and then boom, I go to Cancun, this guy is tattooed and pierced, my knight in shining armor — literally, armor. And I marry him in four days."

Pamela had been in other abusive relationships and was now seeing it as a cycle that she was determined to break, if not for herself, then for the sake of her children. Brandon was "very traumatized" when his father assaulted his mother. And Pamela could accept no verbal assurances that her husband's behavior had changed. "It took 36 years to make him the way he is, I don't see how three months is going to give me 100 percent assurance that it's safe."

She wrote a letter to Tommy and told him that when she became a mother her life changed. Now the kids were her priority, not him. Perhaps she could've balanced things better, she admitted, but she didn't know how. Looking at it without him around, she realized that part of the problem was that Tommy was a very immature person. "His childhood was onstage," she reasoned, citing the fact that he was in Motley Crue, living with the band as a teenager. "Being in a situation like that is really strange. It doesn't make for normal people. It's crazy making." She even believed that all the hard partying and drugs may have caused a chemical imbalance.

At the time, she seemed convinced that it was a bad idea to put her kids in the position of waiting to see what might happen. If that meant that Tommy could only be a part-time father, then maybe that was the best father he could be for the time being. Her goal, she said, was to become friends so that they could co-parent their children. But Tommy wanted to have his family back together. He wanted yet another chance.

On Mother's Day he sent a card. Inside it read: "It must've been really hard being a mother to all three of us."

Chapter 21

"TOMMY AND I HAD a real soul connection," Pam would reflect while he was in jail. "There's not a minute that goes by that I'm not thinking about him and hoping that he's doing well. But I have to let him heal himself and do whatever he's going to do and it can't be because of me, because we've done that already. It's got to be for himself."

Although she was in touch, and been reported to have sent him sexy photographs, Pamela was proceeding with her divorce and was entertaining the idea of dating again. She told Howard Stern that she had asked out Bryan Adams, "but he wouldn't go out with me — he didn't want Tommy knocking on his door." Neither did Lenny Kravitz. (Jerry Springer had made a guest appearance on V.I.P., showing a huge interest in Pam, but, this time, it wasn't mutual.)

"It'll take a certain kind of man for me to ever get involved with, because he'll have to realize I don't have two children. I have three. Tommy is always going to be part of my life."

One man who was willing was Kelly Slater. He had, after all, been going out with Pamela when Tommy followed her to Mexico and swept her off her feet. Having lost her once, he was determined not to let a second opportunity pass him by. Pam considered Kelly a good friend. They hadn't really spoken since she married Tommy, but she picked up the phone after Tommy went to jail and mended fences. "I told Kelly I was sorry and he was OK," she said. "We're really good friends, we love each other and he knows who I am, and all the hype doesn't faze him."

Like Jon Peters, Kelly was a man that Pamela could rely on. As she started spending more time with him, the old flames began gathering heat. Soon, he was spending time at her place. Pamela had since moved to a gated community high in the Hollywood Hills. Tommy heard about it and began calling Pamela collect every day from jail, unaware that Kelly was in the house.

Things were also heating up again concerning the Bret Michaels videotape. IEG, the company that had released Pam & Tommy Lee: Hardcore & Uncensored, said that Bret had given them the tape. He disagreed and got an injunction. Bret claimed that he had made the tape for "solo sexual purposes" while he was out on the road with his band Poison in 1994.

This made Pam livid. "F**k Bret!" she exploded. "Like I need to have anything to do with this stupid video that was supposed to be destroyed a long time ago by a tired-ass loser." Bret claims that he and Pamela never had a discussion about the tape. "We didn't wake up the next day with her saying this tape should self-destruct," he claimed.

Pamela had the harshest words for IEG, however, who sent an emissary to collect an award at Hot D'Or, the annual erotic film festival that took place at the same time as the Cannes Film Festival. Pamela had been voted Best Female Actress in an Adult Feature, two days after Tommy was sent to jail. They sent a press release announcing Pamela's victory in the XXX acting world, promising that she was going to be sued for interfering with the distribution of the tape.

"They've made so much money it's evil, evil, evil," Pam said of IEG. "I don't know if we'll be able to shut 'em down, but I'll be able to sue them for every nickel they ever made and put it in my children's bank accounts instead of their greasy hands."

Tommy Lee was released from the Los Angeles County Jail September 5, after serving nearly four months of his six-month sentence. She would not see him and would only speak to him through his therapist. He was only allowed to see his sons under strict supervision. Tommy was angry about a lot of things and he was not happy that Pamela was seeing someone else and was away on a vacation with Kelly to his home in Cocoa Beach, Florida, to meet his parents.

"It's not going well at all," Pam admitted at the time. "I only wish he [Tommy] could understand what happened but when he brings up the past, when he talks about us, I think, Who are you talking about? He's actually in a very scary place as far as I'm concerned. I left him a message saying I'm happy that you've learned so much, done so much, read so much. Everything can only be better. And I know you don't want to talk to me right now, you don't want to work on our friendship and that you feel bad. But I support you and love you and always will. He can't understand me loving him from a distance. He says, 'You're either married to me or I hate you. If you are going to divorce me I don't ever want to talk to you again.' It's all or nothing."

Tommy threatened to write a book, revealing the steamy secrets of their sex life and promised her he had plenty of photos to use. In desperation, she even consulted the famed psychic Joya Deleany, who told Pamela that she and Tommy had known each other in past lives and had always been in conflict. Pamela even convinced Tommy to see the woman and chant with her, hoping that it would help him with his anger and denial. Of the somewhat unorthodox treatment Pam said, "I want us to get along well enough that we can be there for them. And I don't want our sons to grow up with all the anger Tommy had inside of him."

Meanwhile, Pamela was still busy with V.I.P. She was also scheduled to do another Playboy shoot, her eighth. "This has to be the classic interview," she told Playboy.

Not to disappoint — it was.

Pamela discussed the state of the union with Tommy. "We were like this," she said crossing her fingers. "Inseparable. It's exactly what I asked for. And I don't blame him for everything. I think it's what we thought true love was. But when you really love somebody, sometimes you just have to leave and let him find his way. You're the one who gets abused and then you're the one who has to be strong enough to stay away. It's so much easier to get married than divorced." She rolled her eyes, but decided to talk about that videotape. "I'm fighting it with my lawyers, but it's a bottomless pit. What really sucks is that it's our personal life. It makes me afraid to take pictures, make scrapbooks, shoot videos of my children. Nothing's sacred."

She also fussed over her boys. "When I'm with my kids," she confessed, "It's like men aren't even present."

And Pamela Anderson talked about sex. She said she often went to strip clubs and the guys she went with got ticked because the girls paid more attention to her. She said that women came on to her all the time. "There have been all sorts of opportunities to experiment," she offered. "But I've never really had the desire. I'd sit around with a bunch of girlfriends telling stories and I'd always be like, 'Wow, that's really cool.' And they'd come on to me and say, 'Pamela, you totally led me on.' " She described the perfect male physique: "The guy has to have a round butt, like two grapefruits in a pair of pantyhose."

She was enthusiastic about men who played dress up. "I'd have to stop Tommy from going down to the card tables in Vegas in my dresses. They were a little too short for him, if you know what I mean." She confessed that she'd tried phone sex, tied lovers up with chains and silk ties, and penetrated men where the sun don't shine. "The finger is a no-brainer. I never strapped anything on, but I have used a vibrator. I called all my girl-friends and we had an LPC meeting — the Little Players Club — where we exchange all our sexual secrets and they tried it on their guys."

Tommy didn't get mad, he got even. Toward the end of 1998, he started dating blonde porn star Jenna Jameson. Pam found out when Tommy invited her and son Brandon to a Motley Crue concert in Los Angeles. Pam arrived with Kelly Slater to find Tommy and Jenna in a lovey-dovey mood. Pam told her drum-bashing ex to make sure that Brandon had adequate protection against the heavy metal noise he was about to encounter, but she would not be going inside with Tommy and

Jenna. "I'm not going anywhere with that whore," she was reported to have said. "I'm sure they'll be making porn videos together and selling them."

It didn't end there. By the spring of 1999, Tommy had taken up with Carmen Electra, who had joined the Baywatch gang, while her husband, basketball freak Dennis Rodman, tried to romance Pam.

Then, somehow, the ice between them melted. During one of their conversations on the phone, which could be tense and terse, Tommy blurted out, "You know, Pam, we did have some good times." Pam was incredulous. She hollered back at him about the drinking, the cheating, the beatings. He lashed out that she had him sent to jail. Then they both crumbled and admitted they were still in love with each other and really ought to try to raise their kids together.

A week later, Kelly Slater rented a U-Haul and was moving his stuff out of Pamela's house on the hill — and she was sporting Tommy's $13,000 diamond ring.

Pam had another surprise for the world, but it wasn't something up her sleeve, exactly.

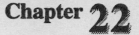

Chapter 22

IN APRIL, PEOPLE WERE seeing a little less of Pamela Anderson. In reality, however, she was everywhere. V.I.P. was cleaning up in the ratings, surpassing Baywatch by some 100,000 viewers. She had become an activist for People for the Ethical Treatment of Animals and was launching all kinds of businesses — from a cosmetics line to a sex advice column on the Internet, where it was reported that products bearing her likeness had racked up more than $70 million in sales. Now that Tommy was back in the picture there was talk that she was pregnant again, that the couple were going to Vegas to elope, and that they were going to get married — again — this time in the nude.

Still, there was something different about Pamela. There was less of her around, particularly in the area for which she had become famous. In mid-April, she underwent a procedure to remove her breast implants. "It's something I've been wanting to do for a very long time and I'm very happy with the decision," she said. "I thought an implant would give me the cleavage I wanted but the pain and the aggravation were hardly worth it. I'm a petite person and having these large breasts just didn't feel right anymore. I think after having children and just nursing, I felt like I was Dolly Parton for the longest time And I just thought, 'I want my natural body back.' "

Like frat boys at a strip club, the press groped for an explanation, noting that Jenny McCarthy, Pamela's Playboy rival, country music star Loretta Lynn, talk-show host Jenny Jones, rocker Stevie Nicks and actress Mariel Hemingway had all had their implants removed, some after experiencing severe medical problems related to their implants. Pamela said there was no medical reason involved, but after the silicone implants, which were banned in 1992 by the FDA, were removed, one of them was found to have a leak. That didn't seem to bother the Ripley's Believe It Or Not Museum in Hollywood, who offered to buy them for display.

Pam declined, but did say that for her, less was more. "I feel much sexier now. I'm running around naked all the time now," she quipped. "It's already hard for me to keep my clothes on, but now, forget it!"

Later, not very long before she decided to be re-enhanced, Pamela couldn't believe how much attention the operation had commanded. "You know how your ears start ringing when people talk about you?" she asked an interviewer from TV Guide. "My tits were ringing. Because everywhere I went people were just looking straight at my chest."

In the same interview, she explained what seemed to be a mystery to so many people after all she'd been through — how she and Tommy were able to reconcile. "We really want to make it work. We have gone through a lot of therapy, personally and together. I just can't imagine being with anybody else. And I really believe we are soul mates. I am not going to make any excuses for his actions, but he is learning how to control himself." She went on to say that he was sober and "there is no room for alcohol in our relationship." Tommy had quit Motley Crue and formed his own group. He was even going to be a guest star on V.I.P.

She described the beating on the evening of Feb. 24, 1998, as "an isolated incident. I really believe that will never be an issue again. Otherwise, I would not be back with him."

In the same issue of TV Guide, Tommy also spoke up about that fateful night. "I was really unhappy professionally, creatively and in our relationship. We just had two new kids and Pamela and I were having our challenges — her postpartum and my unhappiness and all that stuff was all pent up. And man, it just had nowhere to go but out and explode and we both pushed each other's buttons. Things got completely blown out of proportion with people thinking there was some big knock-down-drag-out fight."

Asked to respond to Tommy's version of the events, Pamela commented, "It does take two people in a relationship to have a fight. We had a problem with communication. It doesn't take two to hit somebody. It takes one person to hit another. It is something we have to work out. I think there is still a little denial going on with him."

Had she thought about it, Pamela would've realized she, too, was in denial, but love, they say, is blind and she couldn't see that the writing was on the wall. Tommy had moved back in and the Malibu house, which Pam had put up for sale, was officially taken off the market. They were still planning to tie the knot and Pam announced that Tommy had a vasectomy and there would be no more children. Late in the summer, however, Tommy got the news that his father was seriously ill, and the wedding was postponed. Nevertheless, they were building a new love nest and planning to bless the house immediately after their marriage ceremony by burying her son Dylan's 21-month-old placenta in keeping with an ancient Oriental belief that it brings good fortune, long life and happiness.

It wasn't to be. The re-wedding date was now set for New Year's Eve. It was to be held on the beach, in the nude. But in the final days heading toward the 21st century, the couple began bickering again. During one of their arguments, Tommy lost his temper and smashed a vase. He cooled off and Pam kept her composure, but as soon as Tommy left the country to go on a promotional trip for his new group, the aptly named Methods of Mayhem, Pam packed up the kids and moved. On Feb. 16, 2000, just five years after she had first married Tommy Lee, Pamela moved into a $16,000-a-month new home in a secured luxury community in Malibu called The Colony. The ex-Baywatch babe also drew a line in the sand with Tommy by dealing his kid sister, Athena, a professional blow. Pam had promised her a recurring role on V.I.P., but after she left Tommy, Pam consigned the first and only episode Athena shot to the cutting room floor.

Once again, Pamela called Kelly Slater, who came back to her arms, perhaps believing that the third time would be the charm. It lasted just over three months, despite her claims that he'd be a perfect father to her two sons and despite his proposal of marriage. Pamela had met a new man. His name was Marcus Schenkenberg, and he was famous as a model in the sexy ads for Calvin Klein jeans.

There were three stories about how they met — one took place in Monaco at a function for People for the Ethical Treatment of Animals (PETA). In 1999, famous vegetarian and ex-Beatle Paul McCartney had given Pamela the first annual award in memory of his wife Linda on behalf of PETA, and Pamela was always available and happy to attend their functions. She was doubly thrilled

when Marcus rescued a tiny bird at a hotel that had
been trapped in a toilet. Another account said they
met at a Baywatch party in Cannes and that
Marcus had been flirting with Gena Lee Nolin
before Pam entered the room. The third, which
came to be viewed as the authentic one, is that they
met at the World Music Awards in Monte Carlo.

Two things were definitely true: The girl from
Canada met the Swedish hunk somewhere in
Europe and spent two days with him in her hotel
room and she called off her wedding to Kelly
Slater, which had been scheduled for June 3.

Head over heels yet again, Pamela said, "Life
without Tommy is better. I wish him well in his life
and I hope he gets the help he needs. I've moved on
with my life. No more reunions, I can guarantee it."

She was definitely moving onward and upward
with her life, but that June, Pamela did have another reunion with Tommy Lee. It was anything but
romantic. Pamela had been called to testify about
alleged probation violations. No longer standing
by her man, she reported that Tommy had, in fact,
drank champagne with her when they were still in
the throes of a reconciliation on New Year's Day.
Tommy got a return trip to L.A. County Jail for
four days.

Pam was feeling bubbly herself by the middle of
summer. She had introduced Marcus to her father

Barry, who must've taken Mr. Anderson aside, because the male supermodel who earned up to $20,000 a day had a very special request — the hand of Barry's daughter. In July, he chartered a yacht and took Pam on a cruise to romantic Catalina Island. Snuggling under the stars, he read her a poem and then popped the question. They toasted with glasses of Krug champagne and that's when Pam noticed Marcus had spiked her drink with a 3-carat emerald-cut diamond ring. Pam said yes and bought Marcus a $75,000 Dodge Viper as an early wedding present. She also chartered a plane and made him a member of the mile-high club by having sex in midair with her fiancé.

They were headed down the aisle and Pam was hoping to become a mom again and have a daughter, but things unraveled fairly quickly. The affair was extremely physical. As Pamela told a friend, "I like to sunbathe nude in the backyard and I couldn't even get a tan because Marcus was all over me." People on the V.I.P. set where aspiring actor Marcus hung out a lot, used to scold him for not letting Pam get enough rest; during breaks, they said, her trailer was always rocking.

Anything that burned that hot was bound to flame out fast, however, and by December, Pam was spotted having a smoochfest in a park near her home with old friend and protector, 55-year-old

Jon Peters. And by the beginning of 2001, she had
called off the marriage. "Marcus is a really nice
man," she said "But I'm looking for something
different. I need to date and see what's out there."

Chapter 23

THE FIRST MAN PAMELA found after admitting, "I'm looking for something different," was musician Michael Bolton. They met aboard a yacht during a celebrity party at the Atlantic Casino Resort in the Bahamas and by January 2001, they were officially an item. True to her word that she wanted to play the field, Pam and the gravelly voiced singer went their separate ways before the first spring flowers had begun to bloom.

On March 4, 2001, Pamela was probably bemoaning the lack of a man in her life, but not for the conventional reasons. Shortly before 11 a.m., Pam's housekeeper, Angela Alvarez, made a startling discovery in one of the guestrooms of Pamela's supposedly secure Malibu home. There was an uninvited woman asleep in the bed with dyed blond hair and brown roots. Angela summoned up the courage and asked the woman who she was. The stranger handed the housekeeper a note, which she immediately delivered to Pamela, who was in her own room just down the hall.

With mounting horror, Pam read the note, filled with spelling and grammatical errors:

You is my obsession. I'm not a lesbian. But when I see you I'm emotional and I have angst to give you this letter. You is my only solution in life. I'm

*trying to suicide me with a box of medicaments for
one month*
    Can you help me please

Pamela had been through this kind of situation
before. Shortly after marrying Tommy Lee, she
began taking kick-boxing lessons after receiving
sick messages and at least one death threat from a
disturbed fan who eventually discovered the secret
number for the show's offices. Seeing this note,
she immediately recognized the threat to her and
her children and called the Lost Hills Sheriff's
Department, gathered up Brandon, 4, and Dylan, 3,
and waited outside the house for the deputies.
Inside, they discovered Christine Roth, a 27-year-
old from France. The 5-foot-7-inch, 120-pound
woman was covered in filth and scabs and was
wearing a red bathing suit very similar to the one
Pam had made famous on Baywatch. Completely
distraught, Christine grabbed a piece of broken
glass and slit her left wrist.

The intruder was taken to a nearby fire station,
where paramedics treated the wound before officials
booked her for felony stalking. She was held in Los
Angeles' Twin Towers Detention Center with bail
set at $150,000. A judge issued an emergency
restraining order against the woman within the hour.

Pam briefly considered patching things up with

Tommy Lee after the frightening incident. She was also feeling particularly shaky because her mom, at age 53, had undergone emergency heart bypass surgery just three days before the stalker had been discovered in Pamela's home.

A few weeks earlier, Pamela had met a Greek show business millionaire, 42-year-old Stavros Merjos, and they enjoyed several dates. For a while, she leaned on him gratefully, even buying him a $25,000 painting by the artist Ed Ruscha for his birthday. She also was seen flea-marketing with Tommy during that period, but that was all about to change. Pamela went to New York after the scary incident with the stalker and attended a tribute concert for soul legend Aretha Franklin. That's where she met the man who she believed would change her destiny.

In the world of pop music, 30-year-old Robert James Ritchie was one of the new kids on the block. He released an album in 1988 and struggled for the next 10 years before finding a place on the charts as Kid Rock, a raunchy Detroit singer who merged rap and rock and performed on stage with strippers.

Like Pamela, Kid Rock had been through a tough marriage early in his life and had a young son. The attraction was instant and the couple seemed to have much in common that had little to do with their public image. Like Pamela, Bob had grown up in a small town, and after years of kicking around, became famous on his home turf and found huge success virtually overnight. "Bob's an angel, a lovely guy," Pamela gushed. "Because we both have these larger-than-life personas, we instantly could relate to the contrast between who we really are and how the world sees us. It's a persona, it's a character, a caricature. Eventually, Bob will be in country music singing with Willie Nelson and I'll be Martha Stewart the second and we'll be like, 'Oh, honey, remember when you were a hot chick and I was jumping around with strippers on the stage?' "

And although Kid Rock had known Tommy Lee, Pamela said he was nothing like her ex-husband. "Bob is so shy and so sweet, I can't even think of one similarity except they're both in music."

In fact, Kid Rock and Tommy Lee had been on fairly friendly terms when she attended the 2001 Kentucky Derby in April with her new musician boyfriend. After that, it was pretty much out-and-out war. Tommy had been under the assumption that his latest attempt to reconcile with Pamela was working.

Then tragedy struck.

When Pamela and Tommy finally divorced in 1998, they agreed to share the custody of their sons. Pamela thought that whatever other problems her ex-husband had, he was a loving and devoted father to their children. "What I want," she said at the time, "is for Brandon and Dylan to be in a really loving, safe environment to be able to flourish as little creative people; and if that means me not being able to be with a person I'm in love with, then that's something I'm willing to give up for their safety and happiness." She may not have been able to live with him, but that didn't mean that he and the kids should be kept apart.

The tragic events to come, however, would change her mind.

On Saturday, June 16, 2001, Tommy threw a belated party for Brandon's fifth birthday, which had already passed on June 5. Brandon was delighted. There was a strawberry and chocolate cake, a magic show and, because it was a hot day, a pool to swim in filled with toys.

There were a dozen or so of Brandon's little friends, who had come with their folks or nannies. Among them was one of Brandon's school chums, Daniel Karven Veres, the 4-year-old son of television producer James Veres and actress Ursula Karven.

Daniel was under the care of Christian Weiss, a male au pair from Germany who had to leave the party early to attend a concert. When it was time for Christian to depart for the concert, Daniel convinced him to let him stay. It was an afternoon filled with fun that came to a tragic end when Daniel's body was found submerged in the shallow end of Tommy's black-bottomed pool. Frantic attempts to revive him followed, but the boy was rushed to nearby Thousand Oaks hospital and was pronounced dead at 5:55 p.m.

An autopsy report ruled the death an accident, according to the Los Angeles Sheriff's Department. But since this was Tommy Lee, there were immediate questions in the wake of the tragedy. Daniels' heartbroken parents blamed Tommy Lee for not providing a lifeguard at the party, even though there were dozens of parents and adult caretakers. The Veres also implicated Judy Ziehm, a 52-year-old former actress who'd long ago appeared in the soft-core porn film Flesh Gordon, who was there supervising the care of three other children.

According to her account, young Daniel's au pair, Christian Weiss, asked her to drive Daniel home and she agreed. She gave her cell phone number to Christian who passed it on to the Veres family. "At the last second, he asked me to give Daniel a ride home with the other kids I was chauffeuring. My guess is that he didn't ask anyone to care for Daniel. He simply assumed that since all the parents knew the boy, we'd keep an eye on him.

That was his big mistake. He left Daniel alone. My conscience is clear. I'm not happy about what happened, but I know I'm not to blame."

"It was a birthday party like a million other birthday parties," said Daniel's outraged father, who was considering possible legal action against Tommy Lee. "And obviously, there wasn't enough help at the pool. It's inexcusable and just amazing to me."

Brandon was traumatized, Pamela asserted. "My children asked me all the time why it happened. How do you answer that?" Pam told a reporter. "I have a school photo of Brandon standing next to little Daniel and it's heartbreaking. I know that children should know about death, but to have them go through something like that, with everything else they've had to endure in their little lives, is beyond words."

Pamela was beginning to question the wisdom of leaving her kids in Tommy's care.

Chapter 24

CUCUMBER SANDWICHES — PAMELA COULDN'T get enough of them in the fall of 2001. That could only mean one thing. She and Kid Rock were going to have a kid: She had talked about having children again after her divorce from Tommy Lee, three years ago. But aside from her just-shy-of-a-year affair with Marcus Schenkenberg, Bob "Kid Rock" Ritchie was the first man that Pamela had been with long enough to decide to try for the daughter she said she wanted so badly.

Since Bob already had a son who was older than both of hers, Pamela knew that he was up to the task of helping her raise Brandon and Dylan. "Bob is also a wonderful father and my kids are getting the nurturing from him they need," she declared. "It's so important that two people share the same attitudes to parenting. Children are not there to be paraded for the amusement of your friends. They need strong, consistent role models. Parents need to behave like parents. I won't have my kids swearing. I'm trying to raise them to be compassionate, responsible human beings."

For Pamela, whose own childhood was rough and lonely, it was important to be the best mother she could. "I believe in attachment parenting," she has professed. "I believe babies need to be held all the time, breastfed and to be in bed with you.

Tommy was completely at odds with how I wanted to raise my kids."

Just how clearly they disagreed would become apparent when Pam began the process of challenging their custody arrangement after the divorce. Pam wasn't thinking about those issues that fall, however. She was smitten with Bob. "I love his energy, his charisma, his personality, his talent. He's gorgeous and sexy," she raved. "He's just a country guy and he's so polite, which you don't find in L.A. He's written me a few love songs, which are totally going to ruin his image."

She wasn't worried about her own image, however, despite the fact that to many observers, this Kid Rock character may have been a good ol' boy, but he wasn't all that different from the bad boys Pamela seemed to go for. "My choices may seem crazy sometimes with men," she proclaimed. "I like to have fun. I don't need anybody for anything. A man in my life is just someone I want to be with instead of someone I need to be with."

She was certainly having fun. The Kid knew how to rock. Caught up in his world, Pamela had a few newsworthy episodes of partying, but they came to a screeching halt when she learned that she was about to become a mother again. This appeared to be inevitable; the two had been canoodling since May, often rendezvousing in Las Vegas where they were once caught playing doctor in a casino restroom.

Unfortunately, just one week after the news of her pregnancy became public, Pamela drove herself to her Beverly Hills gynecologist in severe pain. She had miscarried again.

It was a sad period for Pamela, trying to explain what had happened to her two kids, trying to cope with her loss, even as her boyfriend Bob was out of town recording his next record. The grief she felt over the loss of her baby only intensified her feelings about her two happy, healthy kids and strengthened her for what was going to be one of the most hellacious custody cases in the history of Hollywood.

In December 2001, Pamela filed documents in the Los Angeles Superior Court in support of her petition to be granted sole custody of her children. In part, the papers said:

Tommy has no idea or does not care what is appropriate for children of their ages. His life revolves around alcohol. [He is] a dangerous man with a tenuous hold on his temper. He has become increasingly volatile, unreasonable and erratic. [He is a] very angry, unstable man who presents a danger to others, particularly when he is using alcohol, as he is presently doing. I fear for the

children's emotional and physical well-being when
they are in the care of their father.

Among other things, she accused him of taking
the kids on a boat trip soon after they witnessed the
tragic drowning of their friend in Tommy's pool at
Brandon's birthday party, even though they had a
phobia of the water. She claimed that he dangled
Brandon when he was an infant in front of their
temperamental 120-pound Rottweiler to force him
to confront his fear of dogs — all the while holding the door closed so Pam couldn't rescue her
child. The 34-year-old actress also accused Tommy
of deliberately exposing the kids to "vivid and
horrifying" television coverage of the September
11 attacks on the World Trade Center. When
Brandon came home from a visit with his father, he
informed her that "everyone died in New York."
Lee's insensitivity, she said, was "indicative of his
lack of understanding of our children's develop-
mental stages or needs."

Pamela further claimed that Tommy told
Brandon that homework is stupid and that reading
is a stupid way to learn. She asserted that Tommy
was jealous over her new relationship with Bob
Ritchie and had told the kids that Ritchie " 'stole
mommy away from us.' I can't imagine any reason
for telling such a thing to the children, other than

to turn them against Mr. Ritchie and me and to torture them emotionally." She further alleged that he was campaigning to turn her kids against her. "After visitations, the children return home and call me derogatory names they could only have heard from their father."

Pam steeled herself for a major battle. "Tommy told me that if I left him, he'd play ping-pong with my kids, he'd get them as much as he could just to drive me nuts," she said in an interview. "It's about hurting me. That's all it is. I don't know why that's still so important. You might have to ask him that. And he would probably turn it all around and you'd probably be married to him in five minutes. He can be very charismatic."

Tommy certainly could. Not only did he deny the charges, but he leveled a few potshots at Pam. Tommy told the court during the amended custody suit hearing that he had been clean and sober for two years and lived "a healthy lifestyle. Unlike Anderson, I have not been described as crawling around on my hands and knees drunk at major functions." He went on to criticize Pamela's relationship with Kid Rock who, he noted "has appeared on television with a marijuana joint behind his ear." When Pamela asked the court to force her 39-year-old ex to hire a nanny to help raise the couple's children, Tommy countered,

"Unlike [Anderson] I parent the children on my own with minimal help from caretakers. I disagree that the primary responsibility for raising children should be delegated to strangers." He also noted that Brandon told his teacher that he had learned the F-word "from mommy" and that the "children frequently complain to me that their mother is never home."

The court denied Pamela's request to have full custody of Brandon and Dylan and to ensure that her sons' visits with their father be monitored. Another court date was scheduled for March, after a doctor completed psychological testing on Tommy.

Round One had gone to Tommy Lee, but both of them were just beginning to fight.

"When I walk into a room and a bunch of strangers are trying to make decisions about my life and my children," Pam vowed, "I say, 'No, they're not gonna get very far.' "

Chapter 25

THE ACTRESS'S COSMETICS LINE, "Pamela," which she developed without animal testing, had gone down the tubes, but she was unfazed. In December, a U.S. District Judge awarded Pamela Anderson and Tommy Lee $740,000 each in their fight against the IEG, who had distributed the infamous videotape. Representatives of the company failed to make the court date and the damages granted to Pam and Tommy were based on their share of profits from the videocassette and DVD sales of the film that were estimated at over $70 million. If there were questions about how and why the videotape, which the Lees said had been stolen, ended up making them money, no one was asking them.

The only concern on Pamela's mind these days was how the tug-of-war custody battle might affect her boys and she was putting all of her efforts into that. Pamela claimed to be spending a small fortune on the case.

"I feel bad because a lot of people go through custody situations and they don't have the best lawyers and they don't have money. I have both of those things and this is still the hardest thing I've ever gone through. I've spent $500,000 so far. In the research I've done for my own case — about domestic violence and how it's so typical, and the tactics used against women — I've learned about how unfairly women are treated in the court system. It's a real problem."

The next hearing, at which Tommy planned to countersue for full custody, was set for March 2002. By the time it was over, there were stories flying back and forth from both camps. Pam accused Tommy of hitting his kids and touching them inappropriately, while Tommy fired back that Pam had coached them to say those things. Both parties called the other a liar. The Los Angeles County District Attorney's Office looked into the matter. According to Sandi Gibbons of that office, "After a careful review, we found insufficient evidence to show that a crime had occurred."

But the biggest bombshell fell in the week before those accusations flew. It was revealed that Pamela Anderson had hepatitis C, a liver condition that affects some 170 million people in the world. The disease, which causes deterioration of the liver and can result in death, is passed through blood-to-blood transmission, which can result from people sharing razors, toothbrushes and needles. She had been informed of it a year previously and had been receiving treatment at UCLA Medical Center ever since.

According to Pamela, it was Tommy's fault that she had contracted hepatitis C.

"The doctor who diagnosed him a long time ago was my doctor, too," Pamela explained. "When we got married, we both had physicals, we had AIDS tests, we had every kind of test you can imagine and we were gonna tell each other what we had, because we'd just started off our life together — what normal people would do.

"But he never told me." And one day, years down the road, a tattoo artist came to their hotel. Tommy was having another tattoo done and Pamela decided to do the same.

"And the guy said, 'Well, I only brought one needle, but you guys are married,' " Pamela recalled. " 'There's nothing you could give each other is there?' And I was like 'No' and Tommy goes, 'No.' "

After a routine physical, which included having her blood drawn, Pamela got a call from her physician, telling her she had antibodies for hepatitis C. She asked how they were going to get rid of it and he informed her that it was incurable. She could live a long life with it or she could die in five years. Being in a state of shock, she couldn't process it all. That's when she started shaking and crying, thinking that her life was over, wondering if her kids were going to die, too. (They weren't; even though the doctor told her the chances of that were extremely slim, Pamela had them tested anyway. The results were negative.)

The doctor asked whether Tommy had told her he had the virus and Pamela said no. He asked if she'd done intravenous drugs or shared any needles with him. And she thought, not in a million years — and then suddenly realized — the tattoo needle.

"It was the only time I have ever shared a needle," she argued. "And I kick myself for doing so. My advice has to be that no matter how well you think you know someone, don't do it. Ever."

"It still hurts to think I got it from the one person I loved the most — who could have avoided giving it to me," said Pamela. It was all so stupid, so unnecessary. And she felt betrayed. She thought Tommy could've simply told the tattoo artist that he didn't feel good about sharing a needle. It might've raised some questions, maybe even started an argument, but she would've been fine. "He was more concerned with what the tattoo artist thought about him than my health or my life," Pamela wrote in Jane magazine. "Which goes with everything else that happened in that relationship anyway. It's just the icing on the cake."

Tommy's spokespeople said that he had been tested when he was in jail in 1998 and did not have hepatitis C. Pamela seemed certain that he was also responsible for the news of her affliction going public.

"It was very hurtful when Tommy put the hepatitis C stuff out in the press," she said. "It was my personal business and I could've talked about it when I wanted to. I've lived with it for a long time. The question is, who has the most to gain by this news being out there? Only a handful of family and friends knew that I've had hepatitis C for some time.

"It's mean-spirited and below the belt to make out that I'm dying as a way of undermining my ability as a mother. Fundamentally, I believe my private life is my own business, but when the press learned of my illness, quite frankly I'd had enough."

The worst part was that she had been blindsided by the disclosure and had not been able to prepare her new boyfriend, Bob, who would inevitably be ambushed by reporters when the news of Pamela's illness broke.

Telling Bob she had this potentially lethal liver disease was one of the hardest things Pamela has ever faced. Having found a man that she loved and she could trust, something she wasn't sure she would ever do again, she now had to face the prospect that he would abandon her. "I was scared that he wouldn't want to be with me," she said. "But I had to risk the relationship."

She recalls that when she told him, he was "devastated" and also angry when she told him how she had gotten it. "I had to lock Bob in a rubber room for a week, 'cause he was just furious," she confided. But in the end he said it didn't change his feelings for her at all. If anything, it strengthened them. Soon after the revelations, while the couple was making one of their frequent getaways to Las Vegas, the Kid took her on his motorcycle to the middle of the Nevada desert and rocked Pamela's world by proposing marriage.

Chapter 26

ON APRIL 11, 2002, Bob put Pam on the back of his motorcycle and drove south of Las Vegas to the desert. His touring mate, a performer called Uncle Kracker, was waiting in a pink Cadillac with the ring. Pamela happily accepted, but wisely decided not to rush into things. She had done that before, disastrously, and having just gone up against Tommy in court and having the whole world informed of the state of her health, she was still reeling. This did not sit well with Bob, who wanted to elope that night, friends said. After all, they had been dating since April 2001, when they met backstage at VH1 Divas at Radio City Music Hall in New York City. Instead, Pamela wanted to be engaged for a full year before walking down the aisle. Bob was also upset that she did not want to spend as much time with him in Detroit as he would have liked.

That June, Pamela announced that V.I.P. would be coming to an end. Although the show was a ratings hit around the world, the U.S. studio that produced it was having trouble bankrolling it, having lost an international partner in the venture. It was fine for Pam, who had her health to look after and a marriage to look forward to.

"I certainly haven't gone into this engagement blindly," Pamela would later explain. "Believe me, the last thing I ever imagined I'd do was marry another rock star."

As for that first husband, Pam had cut him out of her life — literally. The tattoo she had done on her wedding ring finger that once said "Tommy's" had been altered to read "Mommy's," and then she had the whole ink stain removed through a painful laser surgery process. "It's just a flesh wound," Pamela quipped. "That's all he ever was."

The wedding to Kid Rock was still planned for summer 2003 and Pamela had ridden a roller coaster adjusting to the kind of relationship that is not as impulsive or compulsive as her first marriage. In August, she appeared on Larry King and said her relationship was "in the trenches." To everyone else, that meant a war or a breakup looming on the horizon. But Pamela knew better. It just meant that they were working on the relationship and cared enough to work things out. "We both have kids, we both have issues, we both have careers, we live in two different places," Pamela explained. "I'm still scared to death. Are you kidding? And I need to resolve a lot of issues with that, I think, before I can really move on and have another serious commitment."

Tommy, it seems, had finally moved on, as well. In August, before a performance in Fort Wayne, Indiana, Tommy Lee proposed to girlfriend Mayte Garcia, formerly the wife of the recording artist, Prince.

By the end of the year, Pamela was considering undergoing the only available treatment for hepatitis C. The medical procedure involves once-weekly injections of Peginterferon and an anti-viral taken orally twice a day. The side effects could be brutal — extreme fatigue, muscle aches, nausea, fevers, depression, hair loss, severe anemia and rashes. Nevertheless, Pamela was ready to endure all of it to get healthy. "I want to do it for my children," she said. "Because I don't want to die."

Thankfully, after undergoing a biopsy at the advice of her doctor to determine if the treatment made sense, Pamela received some good news. "They rate a liver from zero to four. Zero is a healthy liver and I'm a one. I have a type of hepatitis that is easily treatable and my doctor told me that he wants to wait. If I did have to be treated, I would jump right into it. I was like, 'You know what? I don't care if I lose my hair and I am sick. I want to get this out of my body and get on with the rest of my life.' "

There were reports that Pamela had taken the doctor's advice about being able to enjoy an occasional glass of wine a little too liberally. Alcohol can increase the risk of the disease's progression and hepatitis C patients are particularly susceptible to cirrhosis of the liver. Pam hotly denied that she was drinking more than she should. "I look after myself and no matter what people think, I'm a very healthy person. I am not this raving drunk, drug addict crazy person — that's just an image created by the media. And it's crap. I happen to be a cheap drunk. If I have a glass of wine, I'm on my ear."

Whatever her personal habits might have been, Pamela showed the same kind of courage and fortitude she had always shown in her life — whether it was putting herself out there as a model and actress or protecting herself and her children from domestic abuse. Despite the stigma attached to hepatitis C, Pam did not shirk from what she considered to be her duty to use her celebrity to spread the word about hepatitis C detection and prevention. Even though it often left her feeling weak, she felt it was important. "It can be so debilitating," Anderson said. "I'm a single mom with two young, beautiful children and I just can't stand the thought of being in bed sick, missing out on spending time with them. I love them so much. These are difficult things to think about. It's hard to write your will when you're in your 30s."

Chapter 27

In 2003, PAMELA ANDERSON finally got some good news. She and Tommy reached a settlement regarding the custody of their two children, Brandon and Dylan. They agreed to share custody of their sons as long as Pamela remains in Los Angeles. She does, however, have the option to bring them with her if she moves to Detroit to live with her fiancé, Bob Ritchie.

The future, as always, remains to be seen. Pam has been taking things day by day. "I'm building my immune system homeopathically and with alternative medicine. I'm seeing an osteopath, I exercise and I'm a vegetarian," she has said. If she has learned anything from her past relationships, it is that haste makes waste. Her children have become her number-one priority and she has learned that she has to take care of herself for their sake. She has cherished every moment, even if it's just turning on the sprinkler and running through it with her boys and the dog. "The kids and I play soccer, t-ball, basketball and we bike ride together. People ask me if I work out and I respond, 'I have two boys.'"

"Everything I do is for my children," she says, again and again as always. " I could lose everything. I could live in a box on the side of the freeway as along as I had my kids." She drives them to class every day, talks to their teachers and has even lent financial support to their school. After meeting a Sunday school teacher at a playground, she began reading Bible stories at the kids' Sunday school. "I want my kids to know how to look within themselves for strength," she explains.

There was no better person to teach them, for throughout her life, Pamela Anderson has had to do just that. Everything has been a challenge. Getting out of a small town and making her name in Hollywood. Learning how to survive domestic abuse and finding the strength to leave a marriage that wasn't working. Figuring out how to handle herself as a businesswoman. And now, living with a potentially deadly illness.

"I treat the disease as another bump in the road," she says. "People need obstacles to reach their potential. In fact, it's given me the opportunity to grow up. The only way I can deal with it is with my twisted sense of humor. Like when I found out, I wanted to make bikinis with pictures of livers on them and give the money to the liver foundation."

Pamela Anderson has laughed and cried all the way to the bank and to the top. She has achieved fame and fortune and the adoration of men across the universe, but the thing that has come to mean the world to her are her two sons and the hope that someday her prince, be it Kid Rock or some other man, will come. "Right now I'm setting boundaries and keeping to what I believe in and having faith in myself," she admitted recently. "Man, no man, it doesn't matter. It's nice to have and if it doesn't happen…Please. It'll happen eventually. I don't care how many times I get trampled on. I don't want to be one of those guarded, living in my shell kind of people. I'd rather keep on getting hurt."

Pamela Anderson began her career as a spokesperson for beer; now she has found herself a spokesperson for much more important things. She was the woman who never had to say a word, just look beautiful in front of the camera, and she has made the discovery that being beautiful has given her a voice. Pamela has become a columnist for Jane magazine in the United States and Elle in Canada.

In February 2003, she appeared in Hitting Home, a British television documentary about battered women. "Hitting Home was therapy for me," she said afterward. "People could really relate to things I was saying about growing up and being in the relationships that I've been in and am in. Especially when people always say, 'Why do you go back or stay in these kinds of relationships?' Sometimes you're made to feel crazy in a relationship where control is such an issue. Abuse isn't just about hitting somebody. It can be psychological, emotional, financial. It just makes you ill how many people experience domestic violence and how many people die at the hands of their mate."

If it was shocking for people to think that the sexiest woman in the world could be so utterly convinced that, because of abuse, she was worthless, Pamela Anderson was brave enough to tell it like it was — and is: "The first thing you lose in an abusive relationship is your self-worth. And I think it is really difficult to leave a relationship when you feel like nothing and you've already been so belittled. It starts with verbal abuse. And by the time it gets to physical abuse, you really have no strength to leave. You feel like this is the only person that's going to be with you because they keep telling you that you're ugly, you're stupid. I guess I felt it was normal," Pamela admits. "I didn't recognize it as domestic violence at the time — I just felt like he [Tommy] was jealous. I knew it was wrong, and I was very unhappy, but I also had the insecurity. It's like this confusion, it's almost like you stay to figure it out.

"It was very, very hard because, first of all, the person that you love the most, the person that you entrusted your life to the most and your children to the most has let you down. When you walk out of the relationship you feel empty, you feel abandoned."

She confessed that even though she had money, friends, good legal counsel and the support of her family, it was still difficult for her to pack up her things, pick up her kids and go. "It's so hard to leave an abusive relationship. You not only have to leave this person and sneak out of the house and protect your children, but then you have to deal with family, the court system, and people who judge you. God doesn't give you anything you can't handle, so you're basically chosen to be one of the strongest people in the world. I have a lot of admiration for people that can leave abusive homes, because when you're ready to leave you're usually at your lowest point. And you have to do it for your kids because if you stay in an abusive relationship they're going to grow up and be abusive or be abused."

Neither the world nor Pam herself has ever rated Pamela Anderson very highly as an actress. It has hardly mattered. She has said that she likes to think of herself as semi-retired these days, happy to be a mom, moving on to design product lines, taking advantage of the fact that she is one of the most famous names in the world and doing things she believes in. Being an actress was never really what mattered, it was just one of the opportunities that have come along and she took advantage of. She recently announced, "I'm so close to never doing anything in TV and movies ever again. I want to build a home, plan a wedding, be 35 and retired."

One project she says she will be doing, however, is a cartoon, giving the voice to a character created by Stan Lee, who invented Spider-Man. "Her name is Stripperella," Pamela explained. "She really looks like me except with bigger boobs and a smaller waist. It looks exactly like me. I feel like now I can eat all the cookies I want because I'll look like that forever."

Conclusion

IMAGINE PAMELA ANDERSON NAKED. She is standing there looking at three lettuce leaves. In a minute she is going to put them on and pray that somehow they form a bikini and stay on long enough for her to have her picture taken.

Pamela Anderson is naked, getting ready to pose for a new poster for one of her many causes she feels strongly about, the People for the Ethical Treatment of Animals. The poster has a cute new slogan. "Turn over a new leaf," it says. "Try vegetarian."

On the Internet, if you want to find something erotic the best thing to do is to type in the words "Pamela Anderson." Those two words actually deliver more links than the word "sex" itself. Everyone imagines Pamela Anderson naked — that's what she's famous for.

As a sex symbol, there has never been anyone like her. She stirs as much sympathy as she does desire. She has lived a life of self-creation and endured the worst kinds of violation. Somehow, she still seems as innocent as a naked babe.

"My public persona is a double-edged sword," she has observed. "And I know I've played into it. The breasts, the blonde hair, all the antics have made me a household name, and I've been able to capitalize on it and make a living. But it's as much a curse as a blessing."

And Pamela Anderson has been blessed and cursed in equal measure. "I've gone through a little public humiliation and things like that, but I believe there's a reason for it somewhere and that's the way I get through it. It's all part of my journey — it just happens to be in front of everybody."

Her journey has taken her from a small corner of Canada to the front pages of newspaper, television screens, and the computer monitors of the world, where she had never shown any fear about exposing herself.

"I think it's been beneficial for me to be open and help other people because I think it helps me," she has observed.

"But I don't think I've ever been one to worry about my image. I remember during one interview when I was talking about hepatitis C and this woman was surprised that I was smart. I was like, 'Thank you, hepatitis, for giving me the chance to form a full sentence!' I can see how other people wouldn't want things to get out there because they're worried about their image, but I don't think I have any image I can damage. It's part of me just being candid. I can't control it. I am who I am and I don't think I'm a bad person.

"I think I'm very free," she added recently. "I've got a lot of pain in my life, but you know, keep it coming. Life is interesting and short and it's not supposed to be easy and if it is, you're probably just in denial."